Rolling
Stonemason
AN AUTOBIOGRAPHY

Rolling
Stonemason
AN AUTOBIOGRAPHY

Fred Bower

Edited & Introduction
by Ron Noon
with Sam Davies

MERLIN PRESS

First published in 1936 by Jonathan Cape
This edition first published in 2015 by
The Merlin Press Ltd
99b Wallis Road
London E9 5LN

www.merlinpress.co.uk

© Introduction and notes: Ron Noon & Sam Davies, 2015

ISBN. 978-0-85036-624-2

British Library Cataloguing in Publication Data
is available from the British Library

Printed in the UK by Imprint Digital, Exeter

CONTENTS

INTRODUCTION

Ron Noon with Sam Davies

The dust jacket on the original 1936 Jonathan Cape edition of *Rolling Stonemason* described Fred Bower's book as follows:

Among the sand dunes of the Wirral Peninsula, overlooking the estuary of the Dee, Mr Fred Bower lives in a hut he built with his own hands. He is well known at the local pub, and in some of the near-by villas, where the small children of Liverpool business-men look to him to play games, to write verses, and to carve gnomes and squirrels and fairies for them. But Mr Bower has a full, adventurous life to look back upon and he has written it in his own vivid and racy idiom. He comes from a family of hereditary stonemasons in Dorset, and though he was born in America and brought up in Liverpool he has practiced the stonemason's craft in three continents, and combined it with such diverse activities as prospecting for gold, and working for the Labour Movement. The story of his life is the story of an ancient craft adapted to modern urban circumstances, and it is closely interwoven with the early years of Tom Mann, Jim Larkin, Philip Snowden and many other notabilities. He has been a prospective candidate for Parliament and worked as a fireman on a tramp steamer, he can tell you all about that dreadful pre-war 'bloody Sunday' in Liverpool, and all about the secret message to posterity which he buried in the foundations of Liverpool Cathedral. This is an autobiography as rich in character as the man himself.

Indeed it is, but the key word to a fuller understanding of Fred's character, *socialism*, was conspicuously absent from the publishers résumé. In 1902 Fred was working on a bank in West Newton Pennsylvania USA when he took up a correspondence course in the Chicago School of Social Science. As he relates in Chapter 7 of *Rolling Stonemason*, 'I ... from that time ... have been a more and more convinced Socialist. And all the rest of my life ... has been devoted to teaching, in my leisure, without money and without price, the gospel of Socialism to my fellow-man'.

Two years later, back home in Liverpool, Fred Bower and his pal, the legendary Jim Larkin, planned a secret message to posterity (Chapter 9), an ironic partnership given that in their schooldays and 'infantile ignorance' they had 'wanted to kill each other' because of their conflicting faiths. Protestant Fred Bower and Catholic James Larkin's conversion to socialism changed all that, even though for over a century according to Frank Neal, 'it was only in Liverpool that the fabric of working life was permanently scarred by open sectarian violence'.[1] On the evening of 26 June 1904 Bower visited Larkin, who compacted into a tin copies of the *Clarion* and *Labour Leader*. Fred carefully placed a letter he had crafted from 'the wage slaves employed on the erection of this cathedral ... dedicated to an unemployed Jewish carpenter', addressed 'To the Finders, Hail!' The next day he covertly laid the tin and its documents in the foundations of the cathedral between two courses of bricks which were 'duly built in' and three weeks later 'King Edward VII duly did his bit and laid the foundation stone over my documents.'

Seven thousand Liverpool worthies attended that 19 July open-air 'circus' on St James Mount, a hill that had once looked down over an insignificant fishing village and later witnessed transatlantic passenger liners congest the river. The Royals, along with the Archbishop of York, Dr. Maclagan, the Bishop of Chester, Dr. Jayne, and the Bishop of Liverpool, Dr. Chavasse, officiated at the foundation ceremony. They sang out the

1 Frank Neal, *Sectarian Violence: The Liverpool Experience, 1819-1914*, (Manchester, 1988), p. 251.

Hallelujah Chorus from Handel's *Messiah* in the richest of all provincial cities, a city described in the *Illustrated London News* in 1881 as 'The New York of Europe, a World City'. There was not a poor man or woman in sight of the ceremony; the bitter everyday reality for Bower and Larkin living down this hill was the Shock City of Dr Duncan and Josephine Butler, dramatizing to millions of unwitting visitors the kind of poverty highlighted by the Rev. Richard Acland Armstrong when he arrived in Liverpool in 1885 to be minister to a wealthy Unitarian congregation:

> I came to Liverpool as a stranger ... to take up my residence in the second city of the mightiest Empire the world has ever seen. I admired its public buildings, its vast docks, its stately shipping, its splendid shops, its lovely parks ... But after the first glance I was appalled by one aspect of things ... The contiguity of immense wealth and abysmal poverty forced itself upon my notice ... the superb carriages of the rich, with their freights of refined and elegant ladies, threaded their way among sections of the population so miserable and squalid that my heart ached at the sight of them. I had seen wealth. I had seen poverty. But never before had I seen the two so jammed together.[2]

But the zeitgeist of Edwardian Liverpool was one of unblushed 'Merseypride' and civic amnesia over the abysmal squalor that had caused the Rev. Armstrong's heartache. As the first person to cut a stone on the Cathedral site and the architect of its greatest secret, Fred, not long returned from working in New York, railed at the physical segregation and social distances that separated Liverpool's wealthy patrician elite from its poor and destitute. These were the stark contrasts addressed to that future society, which 'compared to ours of to-day' would be 'a happier existence'.

Advised not to make the secret public 'till there is so much

2 Quoted in Tony Lane, *Liverpool: City of the Sea*, (2nd ed., Liverpool, 1997), pp. 51-2.

weight built on it that it can't very well be removed', the time capsule is impossible to excavate and remains where it was buried. A locational clue for curious visitors to the Cathedral is an inscription to the left of the Lady Chapel reading 'To the Glory of God this foundation stone was laid by Edward VII on the 19th day of July 1904'. No archaeological dig is needed because the full details of Bower's secret message are fully recoverable in Chapter 9 of this re-publication of Fred Bower's autobiography.

The Merseyside Construction Safety Campaign (MCSC) organised a centennial commemoration of the 'Secret in the Stone' in the Lady Chapel of the Anglican Cathedral on 27 June 2004. This was a splendidly successful public history event, arranged and publicised as a means of ensuring a more lasting legacy for Bower and Larkin. Some knowledge of Fred's out-of-print and increasingly rare autobiography, particularly of the secret in the foundation stone, had seared itself into the local labour movement's collective memory, but MCSC grasped the need for much more than generalised whispers and echoes from informed academics and local historians. The involvement of building workers was also a reminder that the industry that Bower worked in all his life is still one where 'business dodges' and industrial accidents proliferate. The alternative centennial commemoration and the short *Secret In The Stone* booklet MCSC sponsored was given extensive local media publicity, making many more people keenly aware that 'buried deep in the brick of that vast monolith to faith and capital, is a people's protest, a whisper of defiance and hope for those whose history has been buried until now'.[3]

The commemoration event and attendant publicity, including a special BBC Radio Merseyside programme on the 'Secret in the Stone', resulted in former friends, relatives and acquaintances of Fred contacting Ron Noon, the author of the pamphlet. They volunteered their reminiscences and reflections, and the original manuscript of the book which included many

3   John Davies, 'Buried in the bricks', in *Notes From a Small Vicar*, 25 June 2004: http://www.johndavies.org/2004/06/buried-in-bricks.html

more of Fred's unpublished poems and verses. Brenda Charles' (nee Evans) recollections were published in the Liverpool Daily Post as *Memories Carved in Stone:*

> He seemed a gentle figure at peace with himself and sometimes, when the impudence was with her, she would ask him for a penny and he would rummage in pockets to find one. There were other times when young Brenda Evans would watch the man shape squirrels and other little animals from sandstone with his chisel and his hands. Such was his poverty that some of these would be swapped for a rabbit for his pot. Of course, she didn't know then, how could she, that this old man was a poet and a writer and a pioneer of British Socialism who had, behind his serene countenance, a burning passion for human justice. Maybe that was why he would give her a penny because they weren't rich people, these fisherfolk, like Brenda's father, Ben Evans, and the others on Banks Road, overlooking the River Dee at Heswall's Lower Village.[4]

The *Rolling Stonemason* died at home in 5 Banks Road Heswall Cheshire on 31 May 1942, the coroner certifying that the cause of death was myorcardial fibrosis due to coronary atheroma, in other words sudden cardiac death. His younger brother Mr W.J. Bower told the *Liverpool Echo* that 'if ever there was a man who lived his life to the full up to the last second' it was Fred,[5] who at the end of 1933 had already been diagnosed with a debilitating lung disease. Fred had a history of rheumatic fever but was told by his doctor that the reason he had been laid low after a few days employment in a Liverpool stone yard was 'silicosis, the dreaded mason's disease, accelerated by malnutrition'. In the Hungry 1930s a miserable life on the dole loomed large unless Bower could secure a pension through a new government-backed fund topped up by stone-working firms that provided a pension for 'any man suffering through the inhaling of stone dust in the course of his work'.

4 *Liverpool Daily Post,* 15 July 2004.
5 *Liverpool Echo,* 1 June 1942.

In order to assess eligibility he was X-rayed three times and made to see other doctors, only for it to be specified that he 'hadn't it bad enough for the pension or even a part of the pension'. He was told that he had the heart condition angina, and would never work again. So a man born in 1871 in Boston Massachusetts, reared in Liverpool, but scion to his father's dynasty of hereditary stonemasons from Langton Matravers in Dorset's Isle of Purbeck, decided to cross the Mersey to the Wirral. There he acquired a 'discarded Liverpool Black Maria which had been used to carry prisoners', and for a few pounds a year rented a small piece of ground in a field in Heswall, to 'find an anchorage and live on my memories'. Breathing in the sea breezes in his new home, he decided he was going to write his autobiography.

Unfortunately in this exceptionally wealthy part of the Wirral Peninsula the authorities and local residents were 'not too pleased with caravans and bungalows' and Fred was evicted from his home on a couple of occasions which made finishing the manuscript all the more remarkable. At the end of 1935 he proudly pronounced: 'I have finished. My literary Godfather is seeing this thing through for me'. Fred had spent endless hours writing and re-writing that 'thing', submitting it for publication first to a competition run by a publishing firm 'open to anyone', then to 'a well known writer in a weekend paper', and then to a Labour MP who represented his craft as a stonemason, but each time he had experienced rejection and disillusionment. It had been a demoralising and seemingly impossible goal for a working-class man to succeed as a writer in the decade synonymous with economic depression. 'I now felt as though I were doomed to die without seeing my work in the Press', while he was suffering 'no delusion as to the shortness of my days through the shortness of my breath'.

The transformation of what had seemed an overwhelming hopelessness into a literary dream come true was achieved with the discovery of a sympathetic patron, the then-famous Liverpool author John Brophy.[6] Bower wrote to Brophy in October 1935 imploring him to read his autobiography, and Brophy did not send back his 'customary refusal' to such requests. An unusually intriguing letter, from a stonemason living in a hut he had built with his own hands, in a place Brophy knew well, impelled a serious evaluation of the colourful personality and incredible life of Bower. Brophy wrote in the foreword to the 1936 publication:

> It seemed to me that such a man in such circumstances might very well be unable to navigate the usual channels of approach to the publishing world, and might therefore legitimately appeal for advice to an author more or less established. It would be churlish to refuse to read his manuscript. But of course the really deciding factor was that I was taken by the salty, simple turns of phrase in that first letter signed Fred Bower. I had begun to like him already.[7]

Brophy had spent four years on the Western Front in the First World War (lying about his age to enlist) and produced a novel entitled *The Bitter End* in 1928 shaped by those experiences, followed two years later by an edited work with Eric Partridge, *Songs and Slang of the British Soldier, 1914–1918*.[8] Malcolm Brown, a later reviewer of this work, described it as a 'jewel of a book' and highlighted its empathy for 'that most distinguished if elusive of writers, Anonymous'. Brophy, he claimed, had raised 'the profile of the unsung, the uncelebrated, the hitherto ignored' and Anonymous 'he felt deserved appropriate … attention' in the literature of that conflagration. Anonymous versus Robert Graves! Why not?

Brophy's penchant for the underdog would go beyond

6 John Brophy (1899-1965); b. Liverpool, author of 40 books; father of novelist Brigid Brophy.
7 For copyright reasons, Brophy's foreword cannot be included in this edition.
8 Re-published as *The Long Trail: What the Soldiers Sang and Said in the Great War of 1914 to 1918*, (co-author Eric Partridge) (London House and Maxwell, 1965; first published in 1930).

Anonymous with Bower's work, and to use the great socialist historian E.P. Thompson's memorable phrase, he 'rescued from the enormous condescension of posterity' an extraordinary ordinary man's life story. More than that, Brophy's intervention ensured that Fred and Jim's secret message after 1936 was officially no secret anymore. What if Fred had not written to Brophy? How many more working-class autobiographies have never made the light of day because there was no literary godfather to bring such manuscripts into the public domain?

When Fred's 'neat little bundle of a manuscript' landed in Brophy's London home it 'seduced' the novelist 'quickly and thoroughly'. Furthermore, 'Mr. Cape ... as I had secretly expected, yielded to the fascination almost as quickly' and so 'I was able to wire a good offer to the hut in Heswall'. Unfortunately 'by that time Mr Bower had been evicted, his hut declared "unfit for human habitation" at any rate in winter'. Consequently when Brophy headed north for his first meeting with Fred in Liverpool, 'we began our conference in a café but quickly adjourned to a public house round the corner' where Fred's five pints of beer to Brophy's 'one small whiskey' fashioned 'a most vivid recollection of him smiling at a tankard and saying, 'Only for this stuff I should be a Member of Parliament by now – but I reckon I got the best o' the bargain'. At pains to deny 'that either Mr. Bower or I became intoxicated on that occasion', Brophy insisted that he was only writing the foreword 'to indicate what manner of a man he is':

He has made his own education, a theorist who has practiced an honourable craft all his life, a man of principle who relishes without doubts or reservations such of the good things of life as come his way. By the standards of most of the people who will read this book these good things have never been lavished upon him, and of late years they have arrived sparsely and uncertainly. But he has no grumbles. He has lived his life according to the best model, pouring out his energy and good-will without stint or thought for the morrow. He has made himself unmistakeably a man of character, and at first glance one can well understand how this wandering political stonemason has friends of all kinds, among politicians and artisans, poets and painters, journalists, suburban villa owners, and dozens of little children, for whom he writes his simple verses and carves his stone squirrels and gnomes.

Many newspaper critics were not as impressed with Brophy's tribute and 'the spontaneous manner in which Mr. Bower talks and writes', and *Rolling Stonemason* was generally not well received on publication. In the *Daily Express*, for instance, a reviewer, revealing as much about his class prejudices as his literary credentials, wrote:

> ... to be honest, I found it almost wholly uninteresting. I will not subscribe to the modern cant which pretends that a man has only got to be a railway porter or other wage-slave to be a master of literary fascination. A dull book is a dull book whoever writes it.[9]

The Manchester Guardian was slightly less sniffy:

> ... it does not seem that this life is at all a remarkable experiment in autobiography ... One should not complain of a prosaic book, perhaps, but there is a suspicion of dullness in parts of this. But if it may be admitted that every human act and thought has some inherent interest, then this is an interesting record even without the shaping spirit of imagination.[10]

There was, however, a more favourable review which surprisingly given its Conservative links, was found in the *Spectator:*

9 *Daily Express*, 9 July 1936.
10 *Manchester Guardian*, 11 August 1936.

His autobiography ... written in his spare time, and 'discovered' by Mr. John Brophy, is a genuine piece of natural writing. It is too sentimental to rank with the masterpieces of Private Frank Richards, but Mr. Bower has a definite flair for telling a story, and the varied life he has led makes this a thoroughly enjoyable book.[11]

Frank Richards was the pseudonym for Francis William Woodruff, Welsh author of *Old Soldiers Never Die*, a classic book based on his experiences as a private on the Western Front, but hardly a like-with-like comparison with a stonemason's autobiography, except in one fascinating respect. The introduction to Woodruff's book was written by Robert Graves, who it has been suggested provided 'uncredited assistance' in its composition. So Graves a commissioned officer, and Brophy who spent four years on the Western Front as a private soldier, subsequently served as literary godfathers to two talented working-class writers whose works may otherwise have not been published.

War will be 'over by Christmas' and 'business as usual' were two of the most delusional battle cries that were still ringing when Brophy celebrated his fifteenth birthday on 6 December 1914. Similar to many of his generation Brophy had already lied his way into uniform to fight for King and Country but the reality of this 'total war', the barren, unromantic struggle over which side could outproduce and outsurvive the other, was a further four bloody years of fighting. The man who Brophy would be literary godfather to shared the same birthday of 6 December, but on that date in 1914, the only war that 43-year-old Bower was engrossed with was the class war. 'Right at the beginning ... I had made up my mind that the powers that be would not get me to kill a man' and his main purpose was 'to help as many people who held the faith, to survive the war'. There is a fascinating account in Chapter 17 of how he and the Liverpool Committee he worked with would supply Quakers and 'honest conscientious objectors' with 'bogus birth certificates and discharges', and arrange for them to be 'shipped on as firemen' to American ports. Brophy, who gave no 'uncredited assistance' to the composition of Fred's book 'apart from dividing ... into chapters and increasing the number of paragraphs', was clearly impressed by Fred's class-war prescience and principle.

Strong socialist values and beliefs were at the core of his personality but throughout his adult life Fred was not just a strong trade unionist for the Operative Stone Masons (OSM), but a character with a sometimes wicked sense of humour and mischievousness. His itinerant work 'on the toby' and his lust for life and adventure is evidenced throughout his incredible life story, but the year 1895 (documented in Chapters 4 and 5, published in reverse chronological order, which Brophy and publisher failed to discern), is worth highlighting to convey this side of Fred's nature.

He was first an *Emigrant to U.S.A. – and Back*, (Chapter 5), and then in the final part of the year from September to December he was involved in real life-threatening dramas with *Adventures at Sea* (Chapter 4). Those dramas were a tragic fire on board the SS *Iona* as it steamed into the mouth of the Thames in the early hours of 18 September and a near tragic sinking on 11 December of the SS *Cambrae* on its way down from Glasgow, hit amidships by the giant Cunard SS *Germanic* in fog at the mouth of the Mersey. The chronological anchor for unravelling the exact time line to this remarkable year is in the opening sentence to Chapter 5: 'The winter of 1895 was one of the severest', and that lasted from December 1894 through to March 1895 when even the Thames was blocked with ice floes, some of them six or seven feet thick. Outside building work was temporarily held up but Fred secured a job in Liverpool on the Dock Board's Riverside Station before returning to the land of his birth for the first time on the White Star Line's *Britannic*.

Bower describes this sojourn as three months of 'seeing and feeling the low side of life'. Not long after securing lodgings in Manhattan there was a strike when Fred like his dad before him refused to be a scab, and so was forced to leave the boarding house. Homelessness was fortunately followed by lazy hazy days spent swimming in the Hudson and East Rivers, taking box car rides out of the city heat, all before a defining incident in a large saloon near the Brooklyn Bridge obliged Fred to take stock and escape a life that 'would soon make me a professional bum or hobo'.

Fred's sustenance had often come from darting in and out of busy saloons after 'weighing' their form and always when he thought 'the man in charge of the free lunch counter could not see if I had purchased a drink or not'. In the bar by the Brooklyn Bridge, he had clearly not assessed the form well enough. Seeing Fred eating food, the burly barman took him to task, rejecting his defence that he'd actually bought a drink and it was on the bar. 'Touch that and you'll see stars' was the barman's retort and when Fred tried a rapid exit the bar-tender let fly a block of hard wood 'which caught me on the back of the head and cut the skin'. It was really a superficial cut but enough for Fred to go into a nearby drug store and persuade the attendant to make the wound look like 'a big job with plenty of plaster'. Fred then returned to the bar and told the bartender that it was a very serious cut, which he'd been advised by the doctor to report at the police station. Fred's 'con' worked and by 'promising not to make a case of it and hurt the house' he was handed a 'quarter-dollar and told … I was good for a free meal till I got a job'.

No longer a 'professional bum' he signed on as an unpaid cattleman on the SS *Civic* to work his passage back to Liverpool where he got into a fight with 'a one-eyed Glaswegian' who'd been working on the Panama Canal. 'I closed his one and only peeper, but I had two black eyes and several loose teeth for my packet' but it was typical of Fred that he nonetheless put the Glaswegian up for the night in Liverpool before seeing him off on the train back up to Scotland. Fast-forward thirty years and Brenda Evans 'didn't know then, how could she, that this old man was a poet and a writer' and once a fighter, not just for socialism. Behind the quiet countenance of the old man that Brenda watched use the lighter hammer and tools of his craft to carve garden ornaments, the gentle soul passionately fond of flowers, and natural beauty of any kind, was a truly amazing and adventurous character.

This passionate, erudite socialist was eventually documented in accounts of the labour movement. William Hamling in 1948, in one of the earliest surveys of Liverpool labour, referred to Bower as one of the significant pioneers. In the first academic study of the 1911 General Transport strike in Liverpool, Harold Hikins noted Bower's role in the syndicalist movement and quoted from his vivid eyewitness account of Liverpool's Bloody Sunday on that sunny 13 August on St George's plateau. Probably the most detailed study up to then of syndicalism and labour on Merseyside was Bob Holton's in 1973, which quoted extensively from *Rolling Stonemason* and coined a lapidary phrase, 'the ubiquitous Fred Bower'.[12]

But those accounts of Fred were still little more than 'whispers and echoes from informed academics' and the MCSC public history project reinforced by previously 'hidden from history' friends, relatives and acquaintances of Bower, wanted more. Brian Hewitt, a nephew of one of Fred's nieces, volunteered the original manuscript of Rolling Stonemason. Hand-written on its cover is this self-analysis: 'Story of My Life: aspirations and poems etc. John Frederick Bower, Mason, Traveller, Bohemian, Hermit, Socialist, Poet, Writer, Boozer, Personal Enemy No.1.' Turning over the page there is another revelatory inscription: 'This original manuscript of my book I present to my Brother Bill as one who too, has seen the light, and hopes

12 W. Hamling, 'A Short History of the Liverpool Trades' Council 1848-1948', reprinted in J. Dye (ed.), *150 Years of Struggle: The Liverpool Labour Movement 1848-1998*, (Liverpool, 1998), p. 37; H.R. Hikins, 'The Liverpool general Transport Strike, 1911', in *Transactions of the Historic Society of Lancashire and Cheshire*, vol. 113, (1961), p. 170; R.J. Holton, 'Syndicalism and Labour on Merseyside, 1906-14", in H.R. Hikins (ed.), *Building the Union: Studies on the Development of the Workers' Movement: Merseyside 1756-1967*, (Liverpool, 1973), p. 144.

to see enthroned, <u>Right</u>. By the author, Fred Bower, Heswall, Cheshire, 1934.' That was his younger brother W.J. Bower who was there in Banks Road when Fred died.

Brian informed Ron Noon that the manuscript and the large number of poems and other writings had very nearly disappeared into the bin when his aunt died. The supreme irony is that without Brophy's intervention at the end of 1935, *Rolling Stonemason* would definitely have disappeared into history's dustbin long before Brian's aunt died. How much easier would that have made it for the Anglican Cathedral authorities and Morrison's the builders working on St James Mount to dismiss stories of a covert time-capsule ceremony? Gossip had spread around Liverpool from the early 1930s but from 1936 they had to deal with much more than gossip and rumour.

The published autobiography stated explicitly that twenty-two years earlier Fred Bower was 'working in Thornton's yard', when he was sent 'to the Liverpool Cathedral site to shape a few stones'. That Dingle stone yard was where Fred's father Joseph was offered and accepted work in 1874, after returning from Boston Massachusetts. Instead of Fred being reared in Langton Matravers where Joe had originally intended to take his family, Fred was nurtured in a tough, fiercely sectarian and Tory area of South Liverpool. So the first person 'to cut a stone' on the Cathedral site was born in the USA, reared in the Dingle and very much shaped in terms of his craft and traditions by Langton Matravers, the Dorset village that even today claims its stonemasons paved the streets of London.

'The Mecca of all the young Purbeck masons ... was London' and a newly married Joe Bower worked there before a major strike in 1868 resulted in his union funds being depleted and 'strangers ... brought in by the masters from the provinces'. That was the reason Joe took his wife and young daughter over to the New World and why Fred proudly declared: 'I am born American because my father refused to be an English blackleg, and sell the principles of his trade organisation'. That pride in his dear old dad and his roots was expressed when Fred insisted 'that the Langton Matravers of Britain can supply a more far-reaching strain of pure pedigree than any so called nobility, without being cluttered up with prostitutes or tyrants'.

But finally back to the Liverpool Cathedral project. It was contracted for in two sections, 'the foundations to the ground level' and then fresh tenders for the superstructure. Morrison's were not the contractors in 1904, and so the uproar that the publication in 1936 of *Rolling Stonemason* occasioned could not be quelled by Morrison's and the church authorities' ever more trenchant denials. In the correspondence of the newspapers there was some abuse but Fred would have smiled at references to the book being the work of a communist fanatic. Most of the colourful group of people who knew him personally were proud to call him a friend and viewed the oxygen of publicity for his autobiography as a belated blow for the underdog and the underprivileged. Seventy-nine years on from the publication of Fred's classic work, eleven years since the MCSC alternative centennial commemoration event, this 2015 re-publication of *Rolling Stonemason* celebrates the 'whisper of defiance and hope for those whose history has been buried until now', now more resonant than ever as Paul Mason argues:

That message still lies where it was buried. It was addressed to the kids in combat trousers protesting outside a Nike store in Seattle, to the rake-thin teenagers sewing trainers in Cambodian sweatshops and to migrant cleaners resting their exhausted heads against bus windows as dawn breaks in London. Few of us can imagine what that message cost to write, in terms of hardship and self-sacrifice. Or the joy experienced on those rare days when the downtrodden people of the world were allowed to stand up and breathe free.[13]

13 Paul Mason, *Live Working or Die Fighting: How the Working Class Went Global*, (Vintage, 2008), p. *xv*.

DEDICATION

To the parents who bred me,
The teachers who led me
To study, and think for myself,
The heroes and sages
Who died in all ages
For Freedom of Man and not pelf*

F.B.

CHAPTER I

A MASON BY HEREDITY

IN the south-east corner of Dorset lies the quaint old village of Langton Maltravers.* It is one of several villages which go to make up what is known as the Isle of Purbeck. Time may have been when it was an island. But, today, only a narrow stream, hardly discernible, bounds one side, the rest being open to the English Channel whose waves have hewn out of its chalk cliffs several caves, some of which were used by the old-time smugglers, who linked that occupation with quarrying.

The rich beds of oolite stone, a continuation of the better known Portland stone belt, provided, then as now, practically the only occupation for the male population. The quarrymen still work under a charter, granted them centuries ago by the Crown, for services rendered against the king's enemies. These charter rights, handed down from father to son, allow them to go to any land, no matter who the owner, and, for a nominal royalty of one shilling per ton, take whatever rock they want. But they must only open up a hole large enough to get their stone out, and take the shortest route out of the field on to the highway, to remove their spoils. Local landowners have tried for generations to put an end to the men's privileges, law court cases have arisen but the Freemen of the Ancient Guild of Purbeck Marblers have always maintained their position. The result has been that a race of semi-independent workmen is still in existence, while England has grown from a manufacturing to

---

* The village is actually called Langton Matravers. Both Bower and the original publishers make this mistake repeatedly.

a machine-factoring nation. No stranger from outside could, or can, come into the district and quarry or hew the stone, without having to reckon with the lineal descendants of the original charter holders.

Some hundred years ago, one of these rugged quarriers, John Bower, coming under the influence of John Wesley, was converted and became a lay preacher. Hardly able to read himself, yet every Sunday he would walk miles into the surrounding hamlets to preach. His family he brought up to family devotions, and was proud indeed of his son Joe who played a fife in the choir at the wee village chapel. But the Mecca of all the young Purbeck masons, then as today, was London. And young Joe, as soon as he had acquired the knack of using the tools of the craft, journeyed into the big city. In a few years he returned to the village to marry his first and only sweetheart, another quarryman's daughter, who did not even have to change her name, the name Bower, in Langton, being as common as Jones in Wales.*

In London, then, the young couple set up housekeeping. But their young adventure was soon to have a check, for a strike, or lock-out, took place in 1868, and, after hanging out for a long time, during which the Operative Stone Masons' Union Funds were depleted, while strangers were brought in by the masters from the provinces, Scotland, even France and Germany, to take their places, Joseph travelled with his young wife and family of one, down to his village home, from where, leaving her with their kindred, he emigrated to the New World.

Here, after much hardship, he eventually struck oil and got work at his trade, returning to England in a year's time to claim his woman, and voyage back, making his home in Boston, Mass. And here, in 1871, was born the author of these ensuing notes. And, if the reader discerns in my narrative, as he reads, a large trace of what some would call the class-war bias, I can't help

---

* This was no exaggeration on Bower's part – in the 1911 Census, Langton Matravers was recorded as having a population of 878 of whom 176 were named Bower.

that. I am a born American, because my father refused to be an English blackleg, and sell the principles of his trade organization which were, and still are, 'All for Each, and Each for All'. And though my old Dad left me no land or lucre, he left me a nobler thing than either when he instilled into me a hatred of an economic social system which divides mankind into two classes, one class (ten per cent, roughly, of the population) who own the land, mines, mills, factories and means of transportation of the world, and another class (some ninety per cent) who own nothing but the labour power embodied in their brains and muscles. Yes, I am proud of the dear old Dad. And of the stock I sprung from. When I hear people boast of their blue blood, I ask myself if they are sane. If I saw a trace of blue blood in my veins I would be off to a doctor. I am proud of my clear red blood which allies me to all the decent peoples of earth. Certain it is that the Langton Maltravers of Britain can supply a more far-reaching strain of pure pedigree. than can any so-called nobility, without being cluttered up with prostitutes or tyrants.

CHAPTER II

BORN BOSTON, REARED LIVERPOOL

I AM told it was on the morning of December 6th, 1871, when I first saw the light, and the place, 26 Middle Street, South Boston, Massachusetts, USA.* I want to be as precise all through this story as I possibly can, so we may as well start precise. I must have started with a retentive memory (now, alas, beginning to work lazily), for I remember things ere I was three, such as my father, in winter, on a bob-sleigh, with the neighbours, careering down the road outside the house.

Middle Street was short but steep. And every time the voyagers passed up the street, pulling their bob to the top of the street for another go, one of them would leave the trail rope to bound on the sidewalk and give me, safely and warmly ensconced on mother's bosom, a playful tickle in the ribs. That was Father.

A waste dump, on a lot opposite, was a storehouse of broken toys, or things I could use as such. The lapboard house we lived in was perched some three feet from the ground, and surrounded by a veranda, led up to by three or four steps. The first two facts my mother verified for me when in my teens, the last I saw as I had pictured it when I, in early manhood, revisited my birthplace. I also remember, now, just turned three years old, the boat, and the seeming never-ending, watery surround, when, on account of a money panic (or what is now so glibly called a 'crisis'), occurring, and Dad had parted with a half-built house he had been working on in his spare time, for a home, he, with the proceeds, brought mother and his three children

---

* This date and address is confirmed in the birth records for the city of Boston in 1871.

to England. He was travelling with two other Purbeck masons and their families, and they had booked through to London via Liverpool. But, here, one of those small things which may mean so much, occurred. Leaving their women and children in the waiting-room at Lime Street Station, and the train not leaving till midnight for London, the three men walked outside to view the town. Their steps led them to the south end of the city, to the part known as the Dingle. Here, taking a bus-man's holiday, they dropped into a stonemason's yard and chatted with the men.* A gift of a plug of sweet American chewing tobacco and they were pals, especially when the natives found the newcomers had kept up their English union membership, and showed their cards to prove it.

'But why go to London? they were asked. 'There *may* be work to be had there, but here there *is* work.'

A hasty decision was taken, work was asked for and obtained. Workmen's houses were being thrown up then, faster then they could be let, and so the three adventurers rented three houses not far off and returned to the station, gathered up their 'encumbrances', and, ere nightfall, had us safely housed.

And so I was brought up in Liverpool and the land I have learnt to call home.† I had not been in England long, I remember, when I was 'lost'. There is, or was, in Liverpool, a house in Greek Street known as 'the Bell Man's,' situated in the midst of the city. Any lost child was handed on from policeman to policeman, till it was safely at the Bell Man's. The name, I assume, ranges from the time when garnering lost children was one of the duties of the now defunct Town Crier. Here, bewildered and distressed mothers sought their errant offspring, and reclaimed them from the motherly caretaker for a fee of sixpence.

---

* The stoneyard was Thornton's on Herculaneum Street.
† Bower can be traced in the census successively as follows: 1881 at 71 Pecksniff Street; 1891 at 34 Upper Park Street; 1901 at 232 Windsor Street; 1911 at 72 North Hill Street. These are all within a few hundred yards of each other in the then strongly Protestant district of Dingle in south Liverpool. Despite the global wanderings he describes in this book, Bower was strongly rooted in a distinctive local setting until the later years of his life.

Wandering about half a mile from my home, I realized I was lost. I set up a howling. A kindly-disposed woman put me into a neighbouring apothecary's shop, till she could fetch a policeman. Leaving me seated in front of the counter, the proprietor went into the back room during a lull in the business. My eyes bulged with wonder when I espied a counter ornament, a glass globe in which disported a couple of golden fishes. Plunging my hand, dirty with wiping tears from my grimy face, into the globe, I essayed to grab the beautiful creatures. How they dashed about their transparent prison! They sure must have had heart disease through their exertions and excitement, when in came the proprietor, looked at the globe with the water now the colour of ink, and was about to bundle me into the street to be lost again, when a policeman arrived and I was duly deposited at the Bell Man's, to be found and claimed an hour or two after by my doting mother, and, after a lot of hugging and kissing, was lectured all the way home on the wickedness of being 'lost'. I thought it was fine.

By the way, years afterwards, I became shop-boy for the same apothecary and, in the intervals between running messages, filled bug-powder and ointment into boxes. Ruminating on the pleasures of being an apothecary and living in an atmosphere of sweet smells, I was interrupted in my reveries by Mr Swain, my employer, sending me into the basement for a certain bottle which he described. I could not reach the bottle and the maid came down, being taller. Standing on a low stool, she reached the bottle and handed it down to me. I fumbled it and the bottle fell to the floor and was smashed. It was liquid ammonia of greatest strength, and the fumes set me choking. The maid fell off the stool on top of me, but not before I had called to Mr Swain 'Help! Help!' He dashed down, bore the maid up the stairs, and I followed, gasping and spluttering. When the maid had recovered and told how it had happened, I got the instant sack. Unknowingly, he had his revenge for me troubling his goldfish. And so I never became an apothecary, all through unpleasant smells.

But I am anticipating. Soon after I was lost, and found, my parents decided to send me to school. I was expelled from my first school, a Church of England one, for truanting, at five, and my second school, a Wesleyan one, for biting the teacher. The poor woman, tired of my mischief-making antics, called me out of the class. As I approached, she grabbed me, put my head between her knees, and spanked me. I was flabbergasted. There was only one woman who had ever taken such liberties with me. Hence it was I screwed my head round, and bit her leg. She yelled, and the school was in an uproar. Some extra spanks, and I was sent home, the proud possessor of a note in an envelope to my mother. I had been discharged. Twice sacked from my work and barely five years old! I have had a few sackings since, but never for biting the boss. However, the local board school was now built, and here I was duly entered, and passed some happy years. What else could any boy say, with imagination and memory, of his schooldays? Only once during that period did I feel I was unjustly treated by the staff and heaven knows I must have tried their patience sorely. I would rather work at the most damnable job on earth than have to put knowledge into a class of boys, if they were as full of devilment as some of us were at that time, in Park Street Board School.

But there were others. At one time, we had in our class a Willy Jones. The only child of, for our neighbourhood, a comfortable home, he was always dressed neatly and well. His extra-deep, starched collar, over the lapel of his coat, was always spotlessly clean, and we unruly, natural boys used to get tired of hearing our mothers continually saying, "Why can't you keep clean like Willy Jones?" He was a lanky, listless boy, with a perpetual frown or half-sneer on his face, who never played with us in the streets. In fact, all his occupation and pleasure seemed to be in keeping clean. I was seated on the form behind him one day and noticed some ink on his collar. When teacher wasn't looking, I touched him. He turned round and I told him of the ink. Immediately he raised his hand to get the teacher's attention and then said that I had thrown ink on his collar. Called out before the class,

I denied it. I may have done it on some other occasions, but not on this one. The teacher, a dark-visaged, hefty man, thrashed me unmercifully, and, to this day, I can't find it in my heart to forgive him. And when I walloped Willy Jones, after school, for telling a lie, and got another hiding next day from the teacher for that, I felt bloodthirsty. But other things soon make such trivial, albeit, at the time, big things to the principals, pass away. I have often pictured Willy Jones after school-days, becoming an office boy, marrying his boss's daughter and dying of TB, leaving half a dozen weakly weeds to struggle through life harnessed to high, starched collars.

Beyond being nearly drowned in the local docks, and the park lake, on several occasions, and chased by the police for playing cricket in the streets with the lamppost for a wicket, nothing stands out worth recording.

There was, however, the case of the haunted house. Right opposite our school was a house and shop standing empty for several years. We boys knew it as the haunted house, because its last tenant had hung himself in it. Every pane of glass had been broken in its windows. On dark nights we children gave it a wide berth and swore to ourselves, till we really believed it, that we had seen a ghost in the upstairs room where the unhappy man had met his death. One day my father confided he had taken the place at a nominal rental. The builders were in and put it to rights. I had to carry furniture after school to the new house two streets away. It was dusk and I had struggled in the semi-darkness almost to the top of the second flight of stairs with a mattress for what was to be my room in the attic, when a noise scared me. I could not forget the ghost. It may have been the wind slamming a bedroom door, but down I fell to the bottom of the stairs with the mattress on top of me. I was jammed between the balustrade and the wall, and could not move. Of course I howled, but not a soul could hear me. No one came, not even the ghost. At length my father arrived, and, dropping what he was carrying, dashed up the stairs and released me, giving me a wigging for believing in ghosts. The only ghost Dad believed in was the Holy Ghost.

But I was about ten now, and wanted to earn money. By my own desire, I started selling evening papers. But I soon got tired, for I wore boots and the run of news-boys, at that time, came from an even lower paid section of the working-class, and ran the streets shoeless. They seemed to think me above them. My shoes gave me caste, and the other boys gave me a rough time. So I started as 'evening' and 'Saturday' boy at local shops, carrying bread and groceries in baskets on my head, till my cranium seemed nigh cracking. This from 4.30 till 10 week-nights, and 7 a.m. to 12 p.m. on Saturdays. All for 1s. 6d. per week, and my tea on Saturdays. Older men will remember that 'tea on Saturdays' bribe in their own shop-boy days. But I was now fourteen, and must look for a full-time job.

About this time one of my boy chums, named Graham, had invited me into his house to see his little dead sister. I had not seen a corpse before and stood gazing with childish awe at the waxen-looking figure, when his father entered the room with a local parson. Old Mr Graham had buried one wife and been left with three boys, now grown-up, and married, when he took to himself a second wife about half his age. She bore him three sons, the eldest my chum, and then a girl. Old Graham, a grizzled, bearded sea-dog, lived for that girl, and now she lay dead. I can see him now, bent and broken, as he came into the death chamber. Then the parson spoke. 'Cheer up', he said. 'She's in Heaven. It's God's will." The old man, shaken with emotion, pulled himself together. I have never seen such a look in any man's eyes as he turned to the man of God. 'God's will? God's will?' he cried. 'Get out of my house before I strike you. What has the wee thing done to God that He should take her? Is your God a Devil? Be off! Be off! If that's your God, be off!' There was more of it, and the cleric excused himself; and betook himself away. As for me, a boy brought up in a godly home atmosphere, I felt it was terrible to speak like that to a parson. Had the old man been stricken to the floor for such seeming blasphemy, I would not have been surprised. The poor child had eaten some tainted ice cream which had set up complications, it transpired afterwards, but the incidence of the old seaman having a nobler idea of God than the latter's paid servant, roused in my childish breast thoughts which undoubtedly tinctured my future philosophy of life.

Some months after, old Graham, now a Liverpool dock-gate man, brought home some oysters. It seems an iron-hulled vessel called the *Dodo* had been laid up for several years or so in some foreign river. There had been difficulties over change of ownership, or port dues, or something. At length she was brought home and put into the graving dock. The water was run off, revealing her bottom covered with a thick incrustation of oysters.

'They are perfectly fit to eat', said Mr Graham to us boys.

'You don't think they will poison us?' I asked him.

I saw him wince and felt guilty of opening an old sore to his memory.

'Not at all, my lad, the paint had long gone off that hull before the oysters gathered', he replied. 'They're quite safe.'

That night my chum and I went down into the graving dock armed with hammers. Cracking the shells of the heap of oysters the ship scalers had already knocked oft, we had the feast of our lives and filled a couple of pillow-cases with others to take home. My parents promptly flung my spoils into the ash midden. They were taking no chances. During the night my little stomach began to give me some qualms. I thought of the little girl who had been poisoned. Was I to meet the same fate? However, it was but the natural corollary of a huge epicurean feast interfering with a digestion accustomed only to modest plain food, and next morning we truanted and found our way back to the dock. Alas! the evening papers had broadcast the news, and the dock was besieged with men and boys, loading bags with the shellfish as the scalers chipped them off in chunks, and with the memory of the gorgeous feast we had had the night before, we had to be satisfied.

Looking back on those childhood days in our 'four-roomed

brick box, with slate lids', with our patient, hardworking mother 'doing' for eight of us, I can only wonder how she managed it. Certainly there was nothing wasted. No married couple in the world spent less on themselves than my dear old parents. Dad, being an exceptionally able and conscientious hard-working man, was lucky in being in pretty steady employment. He had no hobbies but was fond of music and a red letter day in our lives was when a van stopped at the door and a mysterious box was left addressed to Dad. How we elder children awaited his homecoming to discover its secret. In due course he came home, toil-worn and weary as usual. To him, also, the contents of the box were a mystery. 'Not to be knocked about!' and 'Handle with care!' it was labelled. Mother was busy in the back kitchen, while we watched Dad unwrap the box and take out sundry packings, to disclose a gorgeous melodeon.

Mother was called in to see the wonderful object. 'Surely there has been a mistake', said Dad, 'for I never sent for this', and then we saw a smile on Mother's face. The secret was out, the only secret I believe that one had held from the other throughout their married life. Mother had saved a bit each week until she could send the fifteen shillings to the Glasgow firm who advertised their instruments in the pages of our only weekly paper, *The Christian Herald*.

And we were a happy family that night, when we children were allowed to stay up till eleven o'clock, while Dad (soon acquiring, with his musical turn of mind, the technique of melodeon playing) gave us tunes, mostly hymns, he had learned in the small Bethel down in Dorset. I can see Dad now, his boots grimed with stone dust, entering the humble dwelling. Straight to the shelf in the top cupboard he would stride. Our biggest room, the kitchen, was only three strides across in either direction anyhow. Lifting down the strong cardboard box, he would take out his new treasure, and, shutting his eyes to all around, soar with the gods, heedless of Mother's admonitions that his supper was getting cold, or that she wanted to clear the table to get on with the ironing.

That old melodeon brought more beauty into our cramped and frugal lives than any gorgeous piped organ. And it seemed almost a sacrilege, when, years after, and after four of us older children had more or less learned to play it, its ribs now exposed, and its wind coming fitfully or not at all, it was consigned to the flames of the kitchen fire. It seemed like being at the cremation of an old friend. Our childish idea of folks who used gas lighting at that time was that they were 'well off'. We used oil lamps and our 'going to bed' time was much influenced by lighting-up time. The memory is still romantic to me, and not so long ago I was moved to write the following Verses which may help to recall, for those old enough, the atmosphere of the period:

WHEN MOTHER LIT THE LAMP

As years roll on and snowy hairs,
Denote life's course ne'er o'er,
We old folks love to muse upon
Sweet childhood's days of yore,
But one thing that stood out alone,
Our playtime seemed to cramp,
We knew 'twas nearly bed-time,
When Mother lit the lamp.

When, after supper, Dad would stretch
Himself upon the couch,
Proceed to fill his pipe out of
His old tobacco pouch,
Whilst Mother'd clear the tea-things,
Us kids would round her scamp,
But we knew our playing time was o'er,
When Mother lit the lamp.

Go sing about your 'lectric lights,
Acetylene and gas,

And others, that discovered are,
As on the years do pass,
But leave to me my musing moods,
My recollections dear,
Of brothers, sisters, scattered now,
In countries, far and near.
Grown old apace, in life's hard race,
And scarred with labour's stamp,
Yet memory oft reviews the scene,
When Mother lit the lamp.

Ah! oft in life's declining years,
We've sat in darkening room,
And essayed to prolong day's light
Whilst hating even's gloom,
But little thought we, once, it did
Life's season-ticket stamp,
When Father on the sofa slept,
And Mother lit the lamp.

CHAPTER III

I BECOME A MASON

MY first job on leaving school was at the apothecary's mentioned earlier. Then, in rapid succession, I became an errand boy in a dyer's and cleaner's, a butcher's boy, and a baker's errand boy. I am afraid I wasn't a useful worker to any of them. The dyer's I got sacked from, for laziness in carrying messages. I would forget I was a son of toil, if there was a building on fire, or a row on. The butcher came to the conclusion he could run his business without me. In fighting, in the slaughter-house attached to his business, with another boy, about whose turn it was for the pig's bladder, I upset a tray of pig's blood which was on order for black puddings. The baker risked bankruptcy by sacking me for staying to play a friendly game of marbles in the street with another errand boy, while gathering his customer's dough. It was a common custom in Liverpool at that time, now practically dead, for customers to buy flour and yeast and knead their own dough at their houses. This we bakers' boys would call for, returning it late the same night or early next morning in the shape of crisp, home-made loaves. I am afraid some folks had some rough heavy tack when I carried the dough and met another errand boy good for a game of marbles. The milkman, who next took me for a hireling, was a cheerful soul whose musical 'Milk-O!' I can seem to hear now. My job was to skip off the low float and deliver the milk as we came to the customers' houses on the round. Some boys mocked him to anger one day, and, giving me the horse whip, he sent me to 'larrop them'. After running in and out of side streets for half a mile, they halted and awaited my onslaught. I hadn't much stomach for the job, and was soon outnumbered, returning with a bloody nose and minus the whip, to be sacked on the spot for losing the whip.

Then it was that the sea called me, as it does at some time or other most seaport boys, and, saying nothing to my parents, and good-bye to my street mates, I crept aboard a ship bound to South America. It was night when I hid myself in the chain locker and soon was fast asleep. How long I slept I knew not, but I felt it must have been days. I remember how, numbed and stiff, I sat up in the dark, dank hole and wondered if my mother had given over weeping for me. I had only seen her crying once before and that was when a long strike was on amongst the masons, and there came a week when the union funds were gone and there was no strike-pay to buy food for the family of eight and pay the rent. I remember how I clenched my little fist and swore to myself I would do something awful to my dad's boss, Mr Thompson, when I was a man, for making my mother cry. And here I felt miserable, as I thought of how I would be doing the same. But, I told myself, I must be brave. I would send money home as soon as I got to Brazil and got a job. And I would telegraph home at our first stop, for I had a shilling saved for this venture. Soon there was much commotion on board. We must be passing Land's End now, I thought.

I was weak on geography at that time. The hatch cover of the locker was open as I had left it when I had stowed myself away, and I popped my head out to see the latitude, and was immediately grabbed and kicked ashore, to find the ship still moored to the quay at the Brunswick Dock, as she had been when I boarded her, six days? – no, hours before. So I didn't stow away that time.

Sheepishly, I faced home and a beating for being out all night and, soon after, started to learn to be a joiner. My first boss was a good enough man in his way but I was simply a cheap labourer to him, my main job being to haul a timber handcart around the town, with a strong donkey load of timber on it. Liverpool is a town over-furnished with gradients, and mine was hard graft, such as boys have more sense than to do today, or bosses have the effrontery to ask them to. There was a rivalry between two private horse-bus services in those days and the rivals would pull up in front of each other to steal passengers, then off again to try to overtake the other bus and steal more passengers. Trying to overtake an opposition bus, one of them caught the hub of my offside wheel and I let go of the single centre shaft, or handle, to save myself. The handle swung around and crashed through the window of the bus. Screams ensued, crowds gathered, and in the hubbub I went home, saying nothing. That evening the boss came round to know was I killed. It seems the crowd had not seen me disappear up a side street, and were looking for my body amongst the smash, after which a policeman had taken the handcart on which there was no name or address, and the timber, to the local lock-up. Again I got the sack, for 'not looking where I was going', as the boss declared.

Soon after this, a breakdown in health sent my Dad down to his village home in Dorset to recuperate. And then a letter came asking Mother and me to come down. Arrived there, I found my uncle had said he would take me into his quarry and teach me to use the tools. This was great news and I spent a happy enough three months. My parents had returned home, but I found plenty of companions and was never happier than when I was exploring the caves or bathing and fishing from the cliffs. On Sundays, my usual pleasure was to escort my old grandfather, carrying his huge Bible with extra large lettering, as he trudged over the countryside. He was a wonderful old man, over eighty, and never seemed weary as I prattled of the wonderful sights of Liverpool. Sometimes he would become reminiscent himself and I well remember how proud I felt of him when he told me of how, things being bad, and the Crimean War on, he had taken his oldest son, a youth of fourteen or so, and, carrying their tools on their shoulders, crossed right over England to Cardiff where work was to be had. My father, being younger, had been left at home, where he was employed scaring crows, for which he received one quartern loaf per week. Arrived at Cardiff, they were met by some masons who explained they had formed a branch of the Masons' Union and were on strike. The two travellers had not known there was a strike on, but that was enough. They were not the sort of men to help the bosses to down their own class. A night's rest and a good breakfast was found for them and off they set back across England. That was the only journey out of Purbeck the old man ever made. However, when he and I arrived at the village where he was to lay preach, I was introduced to the brethren somewhat as follows:

'This be Joe's son, 'snow, from Liverpool. Beant bin yer long. Cast know what he dost say? I casn't ver well,' and so on. At such times, listening to and trying to understand their broad Dorset dialect, I almost felt like a foreigner. But those were happy days, as, in the darkening evening, my aged grandsire described the ways of the birds and beasts whose nocturnal noises broke on our ears as we ambled back to home and bed.

The method of working the quarries there is different from the 'cut and fill up' principle in Portland, and elsewhere. Unlike the cliff quarries, where the refuse is tipped into the sea, the inland quarries are a series of mammoth rabbit holes. An inclined plane leads to the mouth of the quarry which is entered by a passage just high enough for a man to stand up in, if not over tall. Like moles, the quarrymen take the stone from in front of them. The stone runs in three beds, each varying in thickness, with an intervening clayish deposit. This deposit is raked out, wedges introduced into the fissure on top, and hammered till a piece breaks off. This piece is then secured to a strong wooden bogie. The quarrier harnesses himself to the truck and drags it, just like a horse, to the foot of the incline. Here, a chain is fastened to the truck or bogie. The other end of the chain is attached to a windlass on top, in which a long pole is inserted. At the outer end of this pole, or spack, as it is called, a donkey or mule is harnessed. The animal goes round and round. Each time it comes to the opening leading down into the quarry, it steps over the chain. At length the chain reaches to the top of the windlass and the donkey boy holds an iron bar against it, in such a way as to turn it back on to itself; when it starts to travel down the windlass again. By the time it has wrapped itself about three times around the windlass, the truck with the piece of stone roped or chained to it, has arrived on the surface. Here, the donkey is released, the stone thrown off to be cut up and shaped, and the chain re-affixed to the bogie, when a man, or boy, pushes it over the edge of the incline, whilst another holds on to a small piece of chain which is used as a brake to ease its progress down the declivity.

In the quarry, the top stratum, about two or three inches thick of stone, is left to form the roof. The rubbish is built up to form pillars, at periods, to uphold this roof. In places, the soil above this roof is so sparse that sheep can be heard overhead, tearing the grass up. Sometimes these roofs sag and form hollows which collect pools of water which percolate down, and the quarriers work ankle-deep in water. There is, however, no gas, and the men work with tallow candles stuck into clay and fastened on to the sides of the working. One can see that it is impossible to get out any very large pieces of rock this way. When larger pieces than usual are required, therefore, these are got from the cliff quarries, where the size is only governed by the mechanical power in use to remove them. It was through sending down the empty truck (as my uncle was ascending the incline up the rough steps hewn in the rock), with the brake chain wrongly adjusted, leaving me with no power to check the truck's progress, that I was sent back to Liverpool next day in disgrace. Had it jumped the track which its wheels had made in its rocky bed throughout many years, he would have been killed. He was an aged man, and a timid one, and didn't intend to take any more chances.

Back in Liverpool, I started in earnest to learn my craft as a mason. I soon picked up the rudiments and, being pretty hefty, could soon turn out a fair day's work in the rougher class. About this time I felt the call of the drum and joined 'the Widow's Army', but only the amateur section, in other words, the local Volunteers. Garbed in my red-striped pants and broidered tunic with a pork-pie-shaped forage cap, on which a metal replica of a bursting grenade was fastened, I was as proud of myself as a peacock. I was Gunner Bower of Battery B in the 6th Lancs.

Artillery.

Time came when we were camped at Altcar, a few miles out of Liverpool. Here my chum and I dodged duty and roamed the sand hills and beach, when – he had an inspiration. Stealing back to the deserted camp (the men being busy on the ranges), he got a couple of candles. Gathering some crabs from beneath the stones on the beach, we stuck a fraction of candle on each one's back and set them down several rabbit holes, after blocking, with our pork-pie hats and tunics, as many holes as we could. Then we squatted, each by a hole, and waited to grab the rabbits, as, scared by the oncoming eerie light-bearer, they would bolt for safety into the open air. But – no rabbits emerged, and, after some ten minutes waiting in breathless suspense, I looked behind me to find the star grass (which the government had planted to keep back the wind-blown sand) had caught fire. The crabs had turned back and set the place afire. Faster than we could stamp it out, the dried grass crackled, and we left it to the crabs and hooked off. The boys were called in off the range to subdue the flames, and a reward offered for the detection of the criminals who set the fire going. But I guess the poor crabs were beyond all retribution.

A mason can never be said to have learned his job, for he might be fifty years at the trade and then get a piece of stone to hew in a shape, and a way, he has never seen before. However, I shifted about, up and down the country, picking up experience all the while. I had joined the union before I was a journeyman, and took great interest in its workings. I noticed that most of the thankless work, such as spokesman for the men at interviewing bosses, etc., was done by one or two individuals in each lodge or branch. And these men couldn't seem to hold a job down for long. These, I found, were the most fearless and independent-minded of my fellow-members. Yet they did not seem to suit the bosses. Not that they were inefficient workmen. Taking it all and all, they were of the best, both in the quality and quantity of their output. But – they had visions. The world would not call them religious men, but they were the really religious men. The men who really believed Heaven could come on this earth, but that it could only be by mankind's efforts.

In other words, I found that these men who did the speaking up for the other men, who risked their jobs, with what that meant of poverty to themselves, their wives and children, were Socialists. And hadn't I heard and read so often that Socialists 'didn't believe in a God'? Forty odd years ago, even as they do today, clerics, and capitalist owned and inspired papers, and the two old political parties mouthed such lying nonsense to keep their tools in subjection. And at that time I believed them. But, of course, I was young, and oh! so ignorant. 'No Socialism for me', I said, as I tried to refute their arguments for the fusion of the trade unions into a political organization with the Socialists, to be called the Labour Party. Little did I reck that the leisure of more than thirty years of my life was to be spent in the advocacy of the Socialists' theory. Up and down Britain I travelled, working on town halls, cathedrals, art galleries, churches, mansions, houses, and business premises. Our Union gave us, when out of work, a cheque book good for 98 days, which cheques we cashed at towns as we came to them and at our clubhouses, the said cheques being good for one and threepence per day, with an extra threepence for Sunday, but – only if you travelled. Thus I became what, in America, is called a hobo. Roadster was our more respectable name here.

In those happy roading days, when I was 'on the toby', as we called it (the term 'hiking' wasn't in use then), I had walked into Crewe from Chester. Getting into the town before the yards closed down for the day, I did a hasty run round. No jobs anywhere, so, making for the Masons' Clubhouse (the Albion Hotel, the pub was called), I collected my tramping money, one and threepence, gave the landlord sixpence for my bed in an attic, and spent the rest. The next morning, as I was washing in the back kitchen, a customer came into the bar. On the kitchen fire two frizzling chops sputtered in a frying pan. Hastily wiping myself donned my coat and cap and strode through the kitchen. Grabbing one of the chops off the pan as I passed, I thrust it into my coat pocket, passed through the pub, wishing the landlord good-bye, and put a few milestones between me and Crewe ere I dug out the greasy morsel, divested it of its tobacco dust, and sat on a grassy bank and devoured it, honey sweet.

It would be a year or two after, when a Liverpool football team was to play Crewe, and I took advantage of the cheap fare to run down there. The same landlord was at the Albion. I made myself known. 'Oh, yes', he said, 'he remembered the tramp mason pinching the chop. But it wasn't mine.' 'No?' I queried. 'Oh, no. It was the missus's. When she came downstairs, I had eaten mine,' he said. I had committed the crime of crimes. Stolen from a woman! But how was I to know? 'Anyhow, how could he tell it was the missus's?' I asked. 'When there's only one chop in the house, it's always mine', he confided. 'Isn't that so, missus?' he called. And a bonny old lady came into the bar, and was told all. 'Ah well, I didn't mind', she said, 'it was a freezing cold day for a youngster to walk to Stoke on an empty belly'. And – I didn't see the football match that day.

However, I must hark back to my tramping brothers. These roadsters were always good union men. Floating into a town where there was plenty of work, they would attend the weekly lodge-meeting of the union. They could tell us of outside jobs, how the wages and conditions were. If trade justified, they would suggest going in for a rise of wages, or a shortening of the number of hours worked. If it came to a strike, they would clear out, so as not to deplete the union's funds by drawing strike pay. This gave the home-guard (the men who had made their homes in the town) a better chance to win their demands. They were the unpaid organizers of the union. If they struck a mansion being erected in an out of the way place, and there was no lodge among the masons, they were not working there long before they would call a dinner-hour meeting out of which a lodge would be formed and a schedule of wages and hours drawn up. Perhaps some of them didn't mouth much about God, but they acted in full belief that Good, which is the essence of God, would eventually overthrow an economic system which bred millionaires on one hand and paupers on the other. They were the real descendants of the early tramping freemasons.

I suppose when Solomon had built his temple with the aid of forced slave labour, he had either to keep his slave masons whom he had captured in the surrounding countries in idleness, or kill them off-hand. Either that, or let them go, which he did. They were given their freedom and wandered in countries far and near. Thus wandering, they became wiser. They would be able to talk of other places. They acted as itinerant news agents. They would become carriers of folk-lore, tellers of tales and of no small account in those days. Perhaps the present Order of Freemasons grew out of that early road-wending free mason, and the people higher up, jealous of the stonemason's knowledge, gathered in their wanderings, formed their lodges and utilized the mason's trade-tools as their symbols, just as the present day processionists, at the London Lord Mayors' shows, walk behind their banners as Cordwainers, etc., as survivals of those guilds of early workmen, without a real cordwainer, i.e. shoemaker, etc., being in their ranks. But the roadster out of work was as near as possible to being a 'freemason' in present conditions. Free to find a master, or tramp the roads, hunting for one. They sometimes had nicknames, taken from their home towns or due to some peculiarity they may have possessed. They seem good days, as I look back, when:

Our only load as We trod the road,
Was a pipe and an O.S.M.* book.
We had little to eat, and drink, and think
Of what we had got to cook.

But our 'Domain', our 'stamping ground',
Was Carlisle to the Chesil Beach.
From Newcastle down to Penrhyn Town,
Wherever the foot could reach.

* Author's note: O.S.M. means Operative Stone Masons, a union now merged with Bricklayers' Union into the Building Workers' Industrial Union.

If we wrought for 'the Bleeder', on Ryland's job,
Or a country mansion or church,
We never would let a 'roader' down
If Fate found him in the lurch.

And we never bothered too much about God,
Or if He had a Soul or not;
But we fashioned His works where beauty lurks
In Chancel, and Nave, and Grot.

And if the job wouldn't stand a 'sub',
Or the 'Coddy' was coarse and gruff,
We'd let the 'home guards' have the 'smooth',
And went off into the rough.

For, it was fifteen-pence for a working day,
Eighteen for the day between,
And a penny for three miles over twelve,
When Victoria was Queen.

And that was six, for a bed, and two, for a pint
And four, for a 'rough stuff' meal,
And three, for an ounce of twist or shag,
To smoke, when our innards did squeal.

But we carried the flag, where the Union lagged,
In village, and town, and yard;
And many a smart young lad we showed,
The use of a Union Card.

And when we felt fit we chiselled the grit,
Or the limestone, soft or hard.
On Lodge nights got in a word or two
To cheer up the old 'home guard'.

There was 'Big Bill Barsby', 'The Leicester Ghost',
'Ginger Leeson', 'The Drake', and 'The Prince',
'Sweat Lindley', 'The Bender', 'The Silver King',
And many, gone, dead, long since.

And if l go up, or go down below,
I'll surely meet some I know
Sticking corners on to the marble steps,
Where the Angels come and go.

Or chiselling coal in a fiery hole,
Where 'Old Nickys' furnaces glow;
And they'll say, 'Well, Fred, I'm glad that you're dead,
Now, We'll have some fun in this show.'

And I'll tell them the 'Stonios' I've left on the Earth
With the 'Brickies' are solid and strong;
And together are fighting for Human Rights,
Which 'They' fought for so hard, and so long.

When the roader's pay was one and threepence each day,
 One-and-six, for the Sunday between,
And a penny for three miles over twelve,
When Victoria was Queen.

'The Bleeder' was a Cockney foreman on Ryland's job, a library in Manchester, presented to the town by a lady in memory of her husband, a Wealthy cotton goods manufacturer or cloth warehouseman. This, for its size, can vie for beauty with any edifice in Britain.* From time immemorial masons have been practically the only craftsmen, except artists and writers, who signed their work. This poem, by an anonymous writer, as far as I can gather, tells of that fact.

* On Deansgate, Manchester. It took a decade to build and was opened in 1900.

MASON MARKS

They are traced in lines on the Parthenon,
Inscribed by the subtle Greek,
And Roman legions have carved them on
Walls, Roads, and Arches antique;
Long ere the Goth with Vandal hand,
Gave scope to his envy dark,
The favoured craft in many a land
Had graven its Mason Mark.

The Obelisks old and the Pyramids,
Around which mystery clings,
The hieroglyphs on the coffin-lids,
Of weird Egyptian Kings;
In Carthage, Syria, Pompeii,
Buried and stern and stark
Have marble records that will not die
Their primitive Mason Mark.

Upon column and freize and capital
In the eye of the chaste volute,
On Scotia's curve or on astregal,
Or in triglyphs channel acute;
Cut somewhere in the entablature,
And oft like a sudden spark
Flashing a light on a date obscure
Shines many a Mason's Mark.

These craftsmen old had a genial whim,
That nothing could e'er destroy,
With a love of their art that naught could dim,
They toiled with chronic joy;
Nothing was too complex to essay,
In aught they dared to embark,
They triumphed on many an Appian way
Where they've left their Mason Mark.

Crossing the Alps like Hannibal,
Or skirting the Pyrenees,
On peak and plain, in crypt and cell,
On foot, or on bandaged knees,
From Tiber to Danube, from Rhine to Seine,
They needed no letters of mark,
Their art was their passport in France or Spain,
And in Britain, their Mason Mark.

The monolith grey and Druid's choir,
The pillared Towers of the Gael,
In Ogham occult their age they bear
That time can only reveal ;
Live on old monuments of the past,
Our beacons through ages dark,
In primal majesty you'll last,
Endeared by each Mason Mark.

On Ryland's job, each mason as he was employed had to draw in a book, which the foreman held, his banker mark. The banker is the stone bench on which he works. Should a stone not fit when taken to its place on the building, the foreman thus knew who had worked it, and who to blame. These marks were cut, the last thing of all, on the top bed of the stone. An interesting example of this custom is to be seen on a couple of pillars at the entrance to 'the Meadows' in Edinburgh. For this public park, quarry-owners of different parts of Scotland gave free a block of their special building stone. These blocks were worked free by members of the Edinburgh Masons' Society. On each piece, deeply cut on the face of the stone for all to see, is the banker-mark of the mason who cut each particular piece. My banker-mark, an anchor, I discarded after the Russian Revolution and adopted the hammer and sickle, Russia's national emblem, in its stead. The first decent job I worked on after that event was two fancy gateposts for a village church not far from Liverpool. I had done the cutting and was engaged fixing them, when the parson, a canon, asked me the meaning of the marks. I explained they were my banker-mark and what banker-marks were. And the canon went off.

CHAPTER IV

ADVENTURES AT SEA

ASSISTING in trade union activities, young, strong, and able, I found myself in Edinburgh, when a fit took me to visit 'the Smoke', as we called London. I had walked into it from Liverpool, the last time. This time, I thought, I would do it in style. I would take a boat. So September 16th, '95, saw me leaving Leith for London on the *S.S. Iona*. There was a commotion at leaving. A Royal Horse Artilleryman, home on furlough before leaving for India, arrived just as the gangway had been drawn ashore. With a miraculous jump he leaped aboard. His friends threw his bag and jack-boots after him. But one of the boots fell in the water, filled and sank. He had not missed his boots for an hour or two, but, after repeated gulps from a bottle of whisky, he remembered them and charged the rest of the passengers with stealing one of them. To save a row, the crew hid him till he sobered up.

This was on Saturday night. Sunday passed and he was not to be seen. Monday morning arrived. There were some thirty men sleeping in bunks and on the floor of the one and only male sleeping cabin, when at 2 a.m. I was awakened by the cry of 'Fire!'* I roused myself in time to see one of the ship's officers, with his huge beard alight, dashing back through the zigzag alleyway. But it was too late to go the way he had come. Like live red and yellow snakes, the flames were licking their way over the thickly painted ceiling of our cabin, which ceiling was the orlop deck of the ship. We were crowded into one end of the cabin. On one side, we could hear men trying to break through bulkheads,

* See reports in *The Times*, 17, 19 and 21 September 1895.

which divided our cabin from the women's room. But they seemed unyielding. Here I saw, for the first time, men facing death. Some were on their knees praying, some cursing, some crying. And here I made a great discovery, which has stood me in good stead throughout my life. My religious upbringing (my grandfather, as I have told, was a lay preacher, my dear old Dad was a deacon, I myself had been for a short time a Sunday school teacher) had led me to believe that the thought which must be uppermost at the last moment in all dying people's minds would be 'Am I going to Hell or Heaven?' But now no such thought entered my mind. I had heard, and it is true (in any case, with me it was), that one's past life rises up before one at such times. Mine did. And I can say, with my hand on my heart, that I was surprised at the few things I found I had done that I needed to be ashamed of. Just two. A little white lie (the only lie) I ever told my mother, and the stealing of an apple from a poor old woman's stall, when a schoolboy. Looking back, it seems almost comical, don't it? No, not fear of the beyond bothered me then, but I do remember feeling upset at thinking of how badly my dear old parents would feel, when they read of my death in that evening's local Liverpool papers. And, if I prayed any, it was that I would be suffocated first, before I was burnt to death.

These thoughts took only a minute fraction of the time it has taken to describe them. But a noise was heard near to us. 'Burst this door open, for your lives!' I looked. There was a painted door leading into the sailors' fo'c'sle, right in the fore-peak of the ship. It hadn't been used for years. It was put there to be used by the sailors to get to their quarters, when the weather was too rough to use their own hatchway. I had one boot on, one off. I had started putting my boots on at the alarm, but had thought, if I am to be burnt, what matter? Boots on, or off! Standing back, I rushed at the door with my stockinged foot. It budged not. Then I looked around and spied the drunken but now sobered soldier. 'Here, mate', I called, and together we rushed at it. Right near the lock, for which the sailors had not been able to find the key, we landed together, with the strength of desperation in our thrust. The door flew open.

I fell, and was trampled on, but not too much hurt, and, as the sailors picked us up and passed us up their companionway, the wind rushed into the cabin, blew the flames through the zigzag alleyway, and through the intervening dining-cabin. Surely the women were all out? For obvious reasons, there was no doorway out of their cabin into the sailors' fo'c'sle.

Out on deck all was commotion. The ship had been stopped; the hoses were playing. Afar could be seen the lights of Clacton-on-Sea. We were nearing the mouth of the Thames when the outbreak occurred. Now the air was filled with the screams of doomed women. Out of some twenty women passengers, six women and a child were trapped. Those who had been saved had run out in their night attire. They were being exhorted to leave whilst the crew were trying to batter down the bulkheads to save us. But prudery, and false modesty, had been their downfall. They had stopped to dress, and died. I will never forget those ghastly moans and shrieks, or the smell of roasting human flesh. The stewardess, Edith Leddingham, had promised to see a child safe, who had been travelling alone up to Scotland, to her grandparents, and was returning to her London home. She had rushed out at the alarm, then, remembering her charge, rushed back, never, alas, to return.

Refusing assistance from the life-boats which had come out to us, the crew eventually got the fire under. But it was a sad homecoming, and harrowing indeed were the scenes when loved ones found that all that was left of their friends, wives, mothers or children, was a blackened, twisted object resembling a charred tree trunk, reverently laid out on deck and covered with sail-cloth. We had been served out with life belts for eventualities. We could not assist the crew. One must do something at such times, or go mad. I fumbled out my pocket book and pencil, and, by the light of a binnacle lamp, with the swishing of water and the hoarse shouts of smoke-choked seamen and echoes of the now ended moans of the poor victims in my ears, I wrote my first poem.

THE FIRE ON THE *IONA*

From Leith, a town in Scotland,
One fine September night,
A steamer, the *Iona*,
Sailed with her human freight.
She was bound for London City,
And all was bright and well,
In fact, all seemed as merry as
The proverbial marriage bell.

The voyage was near ending,
All had retired to rest,
And all was peace and quiet,
Where late was laugh and jest,
That night when off the Gunfleet,
When all was smooth and calm,
Save the throbbing of the engines,
Like the pulse's beating qualm.

A cry of terror rang around
The ship, from stem to stern,
The passengers awoke in haste,
The horrid truth to learn.
A grand but truly awful sight,
Is a ship on fire at sea.
I've seen it only once, but that
Was once too oft for me.

The passengers stood, helpless, back,
Their aid not in demand,
'Thank God the Women are all out'
Was heard on every hand.
But, stop! where is the stewardess?
And other Women, five,
A little child as well, Good God!
The workers fiercer strive.

But all, alas, of no avail,
To enter there is death,
E'en now the crew are struggling
And gasping for their breath.
And when next morn at daylight
The flames were quite subdued,
Ah, horrid sight, the cabin floor
With corpses was bestrewed.

Sad, sad indeed, the landing,
For soon the truth got round,
And husbands there were waiting
For wives who ne'er were found.
And fathers for their daughters,
And lovers for their loved,
Alas, their souls had hurried
To brighter realms above.

So, bring out your books of glory,
Of honour and renown,
And let the name of Leddingham be
For ever handed down.
She had been seen in safety,
Yet rushed back in the room,
To save a child, alas, too late!
That act had been her doom.
But – along with brave Grace Darling,
And Miss Florence Nightingale,
Her name shall be remembered
Till memory, tottering, fail.

This poem, as I said, my first, and rather crude, I started on the
ship, but finished after landing.

An inquest was duly held.* I was summoned and gave my evidence. So did Mac, the soldier. It was adjourned for a week which I spent with Mac at the Woolwich Barracks. Here I was rigged in canvas overalls and acted as an orderly, brushing up and dodging the officers. I had spent a couple of years in the 'Widow's Army', or, rather Volunteers, and knew the salutes. The papers made a fuss of Mac, and the officers were quite proud of him. Eventually, the inquest over, I returned with Mac and we spent our fees, four and sixpence each, with the boys at the canteen.

But I couldn't sleep o' nights. Each night, no matter what time I went to bed, at exactly two o'clock in the morning I would awake bathed in perspiration. I was living the experience over again. The officers of the *Iona* had told me, after I had given my evidence, that I had been very fair. 'Letters to the Editor' had been appearing in the London papers, almost charging the crew with cowardice. My evidence had shown how absolutely hopeless was any effort that could have been made to get into the women's cabin once the flames had closed the passage. 'Any time you wish to go back to Scotland, you can have a free trip with us', said the first mate. A few days after, therefore, I got to the dock only to find the *Iona* steaming away for the north, and now in mid-river.

One place is as good as another, I thought, as I bought a five shilling deck ticket to Newcastle. But this expense left me with only sixpence. We duly cleared for the Tyne. My ticket only allowed me to use the deck. It gave me absolutely no shelter, and lord! how it rained! At last, a door, opening, showed me a cosy cabin with neat, clean-bedded bunks around the side. I was desperate. Opening the door, I dashed in. 'God, what a night!' I said, looking across at a table where the steward and some passengers were playing cards. 'I pity those poor devils on deck to-night', I added. 'Don't pity them, mate', said the steward.

* See *Morning Post*, 2 October 1895. It was reported that 'Frederick Bower, a stonemason, of Bond Street, Vauxhall' gave evidence, stating that 'he thought the sailors did all they could'.

'Most of them have been paid off from ships and are going to their homes on the Tyne, and begrudge the extra three bob for beds. Many of them have more money than you or me.' God help them, if they haven't more than me, I was thinking, when the steward interrupted me by asking would I have a hand. It was halfpenny nap. I took a chance with my sixpence. Luck favoured me and I won ten shillings. Then the turn came and I lost all, even my sixpence. 'I think I'll finish', I said. 'I suppose any bunk not claimed is mine?' 'That's right, mister', replied the steward, and I was soon asleep, not without a thought of the poor wretches out in the cold wet night on deck. Next day, at noon, tickets were collected just as we were passing the Shields. And, of course, I must run right into the steward I had played cards with the night before. 'Tickets, please.' I gave him mine. 'Here!' he said. 'This is a deck ticket, and you had a bed last night. Another three bob? 'I haven't it, mate', I said. 'You won it all last night.' 'Well, you're the limit!' he said. But he let me off.

It was now Sunday. My union cheque book got me one and sixpence. I hired a bed, but did not use it, for that night the old Mansion House by the high level bridge took fire. It was filled with barrels of oil, and half Newcastle must have been out that night watching the display as the barrels burst and sent the sparks sky-high.* Next day, finding no job, I pawned my watch and sailed on the *Bernicia* back to Leith. Here I started to work, but Scotland always looks cold in December, so on the 11th I booked passage by the *Cumbrae* from Glasgow to Liverpool. That ship did not take fire, but it sank, with all my belongings, at the mouth of the Mersey.†

It was about four in the afternoon and we had just entered the estuary to the Mersey, when a dense fog came up. Fog horns and

---

* See *North East Daily Gazette*, 7 October 1895. The building was completely gutted in less than an hour in a spectacular fire fuelled by the oil rig kept there, and further exacerbated by the bitumen stored in the adjoining building.

† See *Manchester Guardian*, 12 December 1895. Bower's account tallies with the report, even down to the theatre company's 'Saved from the Sea' and Lord Dunraven's speech.

syrens were sounding all about us. At half-speed our boat crept through the opaque blanket. The novelty and possible danger kept me on deck, when, standing on the poop, l discerned a towering liner heading straight across our beam. Both boats put their engines full steam astern, but I had just time to read her name *Germanic* when the ship's way carried her forward to crash into us amidships, cleaving our boat in two. The noise resembled nothing more than a huge shattering of crockery, while the small boat quivered like a live thing.

From where I stood, grasping the rails, it seemed like looking up the side of a house, the liner's bows overhanging half the *Cumbrae*. With others, I jumped at, and caught, the huge links of the bow anchor chain, and went hand over hand up, to be grasped and pulled on board by willing hands. The liner had, meanwhile, dropped two boats which picked up some who had jumped into the sea, and took off the rest who had run aft as we collided. The only casualty was one woman who had fallen at the impact, and smashed some ribs. The liner sent down a sail basket, and she was safely hauled aboard.

Safe on the liner's deck, I could look on the scenes of rescue. One sight, which will always stay with me, was of a white-haired old man with his daughter, waiting their turn to be handed into the boat. With their arms about each other, and a look of absolute submission to the will of God, they would have made the subject for a noble picture. She was coming to Liverpool to embark for South America, to marry a Scottish lover who had made good there, and all her wedding presents and home-founding gear were given to the waves.

'Everybody off?' cried the liner's captain. 'Aye, aye, sir,' rang out the officer in command of the activities. Giving the order to go astern, the liner backed away, dragging the doomed vessel with her. 'Shake her up,' the captain calls clown to the engine-room. Now the screws race like mad and the vibration shook the wreck from our bows, and she up-ended herself and settled to the bottom. Our lives were saved mainly because the liner's captain had the sense to hold on after ramming us, his bows acting as a plug in the hole themselves had made.

Safe, the shipwrecked people were regaled with hot coffee and food till a better meal was prepared, when we were ushered into the saloon dining-room. Here, at long tables, set on beautiful rich carpeted floors, we were regaled with choice food and whatever in the way of drinks we desired. At an adjacent long table sat the liner's saloon passengers who were going out to America. After feeding us well, the captain of the *Germanic* made a speech. Our captain replied. John Hare, the actor, who was going out to America with a theatrical company on tour, then spoke. We had on our boat a third-rate theatrical company who had been touring Scotland in a drama called *Saved from the Sea*. It was quite a joke amongst us, for one of these artists was wearing a jersey, back to front, on which was worked in white the words 'Saved from the Sea'. He was coatless, and there it was for all to see.

We listened to a speech by Lord Dunraven, who was aboard the *Germanic*. A short time previously he had tried to win the America Cup with his yacht *Valkyrie III*. He felt he had been jockeyed out of the prize by attendant sightseers' boats butting in on his course, and, taking umbrage, had returned to England, where he had somewhat insinuated the American yachtsmen were no sports. Something had been said in America to the effect that he was no gentleman not to have said what he felt ere he had left them. With a true sportsman's nerve, he was going back to beard the lions in their den, when the collision happened. He spoke of his pride in being a countryman of the men who had so ably taken us off the wreck. After him spoke a Yankee parson. He was going back to his church in Virginia, he said, with much emotion, but his first sermon was going to be on the bravery of British seamen.

Eventually the *Germanic* was turned about and slowly brought back to Liverpool landing-stage. In Liverpool, then, I worked for a while, but after a few months I had a chance to go on a trip to Havre. 'The third time does it' is an old superstition. My parents could hardly be called superstitious, but they liked not the idea of my going. I knew my mother was fretting about it, and, the night before sailing, lying in my bed, and I could swear I was awake, albeit in darkness, I saw a woman's arm between me and the ceiling. It seemed to me to be a portent bidding me stay at home. But I knew, if I heeded the admonition, never more would I venture on water. If it had to be, it had, I felt, and so we sailed. Certainly the old S.S. *Phoenician* had a rather rough time, for leaving port we ran into rough weather, the cargo had shifted and she nosed and dived quite some as we skirted the Welsh coast, but she made Havre, and, leaving us in France, went on to Valparaiso. In a fortnight we returned to Liverpool and I had squashed for ever in my mind the bogy that 'the third time does it'.

CHAPTER V

EMIGRANT TO USA – AND BACK

THE winter of 1895 was one of the severest. All outside building work was held up through frost. However I had secured work at the Liverpool Dock Board's Riverside Station, which was being built for trains to carry passengers' direct off the deep-water boats to London, in order to compete with the Southampton traffic. The work had to be pushed on. Working there one day, I was accosted by a chap with a Yankee drawl, wanting to know if I would buy a ticket 'to the States'. It seemed he was a young American who had got himself stranded in Liverpool. His mother had sent him a ticket for use on any White Star boat for three months ahead. But he had just signed on as a sailor on a boat leaving England that night. He wanted a few shillings for a beano with the boys at the lodging-house where he had been staying, to commemorate his departure. I took a chance on the ticket being a dud, or stolen, and gave him one pound for it.

Behold me then, a few weeks after, under the name of John Thomas O'Neill, aboard the *Britannic,* sister ship to the *Germanic,* sailing to the land of my birth. We had no sooner left Liverpool than all hands on board were herded together to answer a roll-call. There were detectives on board to arrest a man named Cross who was wanted by the police. In alphabetical order the names of the steerage passengers were called out. A and B and so on had been dealt with. It came to O. 'John Thomas O'Neill' called the purser's assistant. I had a momentary lapse. I forgot the part I was playing. 'John Thomas O'Neill! John Thomas O'Neill!' he reiterated. Then it dawned on me. 'Here!' I called. 'Why don't you answer?' he said. 'Have you forgotten your name?' Little did he think I had.

So, day by day, till we reached New York, were the names called out, but no Mr. Cross materialized, and it was conjectured he must have 'jumped into the ditch' between Liverpool and Queenstown. At the latter place more steerage passengers were embarked and we took off again. The weather was a bit rough and many of the Irish colleens were seasick. To one of them I acted as gallant, and we got very pally. The different nationalities, I observed, kept together, but everybody thought I was an Irishman. Didn't I answer to John Thomas O'Neill every day? So I played twenty-fives, or danced to the Irish fiddler, and it wasn't till they saw me eating meat on the Friday, that they felt I wasn't one of them. At eight o'clock each night the sexes were segregated. A good idea, no doubt, for all observant people will testify how amorous most people, not deep-rooted, can become on a sea voyage. A couple of days after leaving Queenstown, I heard two of my fellow Irishmen, who had come aboard at Queenstown, talking of the fun they had with the girls, the night before, after eight o'clock. I chipped in, and they told me the 'how' of it.

I told my colleen I would be with her at the stern, about ten past eight. The single men were berthed forward. 'All women aft!' came the eight o'clock command. The lighted alleyways were blocked by an iron fold-up gate guarded by a quartermaster. Going up to him, I asked for the ship's surgery, which I knew was aft. He pointed along the alleyway and watched me just before I got to it, I looked back. He was watching me just when I should have sheered off to where, in the semidarkness, waited my colleen. I had no alternative but to enter the surgery door. 'Well?' said the ship's doctor, 'What's the matter with you?' I pulled myself together. 'Tummy ache,' I replied. 'Ah, we'll soon fix that!' And he poured out, and stood by whilst I swallowed, the heaviest black draught I ever tackled. 'You'll be all right in the morning.' 'I hope so,' I said, with a wry face, as I emerged into the alleyway to hear the quartermaster holloa 'Hi! This way!' And back I had to go, to my own end of the ship. The next day I was too busy with my own pressing affairs to speak to the colleen. In fact I never spoke to her any more. I had suffered enough for love.

However, New York reached, I was allowed ashore without the necessity of going through Ellis Island, the notorious clearing-house for emigrants. I had been given the address of a boarding-house near the docks, by a sailor on board, and this I made for on landing. They were a Liverpool Irish family, he a docker, or longshoreman as they call them in the United States. I had changed my ten pounds capital into American money on the boat. The docker and a couple of boarders were playing poker. Would I play? I said 'Yes. I'll have to learn sometime'. During that week I learnt. It cost me just over my fifty dollars, all I had, and I had no work. I had struck a bad patch. The stone-cutters in New York and vicinity were all on strike. I could have got plenty of jobs had I chosen to work as a blackleg. The boarding-house keeper couldn't keep a man who wouldn't work on principle, and I was evicted.

Then I had a happy three months, seeing and feeling the low side of life. The weather was glorious. Bathing from the piers, free, and I could always hop into a saloon and steal a free lunch after I had weighed form and picked the busy saloons at noon, when the man in charge of the free lunch counter could not see if I had purchased a drink or not, at the opposite beer counter. Never fastidious, I nevertheless smoked the best cigars at that time that the world produced. Stationing myself on sailing days at the entrance to the sheds where the liners lay at rest, up would come a cab. Passengers would go to enter the sheds. 'No smoking, sir," would say the cop stationed at the entrance, pointing to a board with that admonition on it, over his head. And just-lighted Henry Clays, and lesser breeds, were flung to the ground, to be snapped up by the down-and-outs. My attire at that time consisted of a pair of shoes, ventilated fore and aft, a thin pair of pants, one shirt and an old hat. On hot days, and it can be hot in New York in summer, I would thrust my old soft hat in my pocket, and dive off the wharf into the Hudson

or East River, swim about for, say, half an hour, then land and
stretch myself out in the sun. In a few minutes, when 'nicely
done on one side', I would turn over and repeat. Sometimes I
would have the idea of taking a run out into the country. Then
I would jump on to a covered railway-truck or box-car, and
when I thought I had gone far enough, and New York would
be wondering where I was, I would get off and wander a mile or
two from the railway track.

On one such day I espied a small tombstone-maker's yard,
some twenty odd miles out. Going in, I asked for a job. Nothing
doing, but the owner was gossipy, and soon I found that he was a
Britisher. His father had been a foreman in Liverpool in the very
first yard my father had worked in. That brought us together,
and he asked me could I use a scythe. 'Of course,' I said. At that
time I would have said I could use anything. 'Then go up the
turnpike, bend to the right; and the third house, painted green,
is mine. Go out into the shed at the back. There you'll find a
scythe hanging. Take it down and mow the grass in the front.
It wants doing. The missus is always at me, but I feel too tired
when I get home to tackle it. Come back and I will give you half
a dollar to help you along.'

Off I set. Somehow I lost my bearings. I found a green-
painted house all right. All the houses there-about stood in
their own little plots and were of boards overlapped, and roofed
with shingles or wooden slates. It seemed a well-kept lawn, but
I entered a shed at the back and found a scythe in the corner.
Coming to the front, I set to, to earn my half-dollar. Anybody
who has used a scythe for the first time will know how I shaped.
Anyhow, there was nothing to cut, not even for a lawn mower.
I had stuck the point of the scythe into the earth half a dozen
times, and fetched up half a dozen clods of earth, when the front
door opened and a woman appeared. I was surprised, for my
sympathetic employer had told me his wife was from home.
'What are you doing there?' she screamed. 'Oh, my lawn, my
lawn. You've ruined it!' Then she forgot she was a lady. When
she had finished I said: 'But, ma'am, your husband sent me to

cut the grass in front of the house.' 'My husband? My husband? Would to God he were here now! He'd kill you. He's been dead three years,' she shrieked. By this time I reckoned I had made a mistake in the house. 'Mr Elliot sent me,' I said. 'This is not Mr. Elliot's house," she moaned. I felt touched, and, stooping, picked up the bits of earth I had displaced, and tried to fit them into their places. I almost cried with her, and eventually got away, but it was too soon to report at the yard in the village, so I did a detour to kill time. Eventually I showed up. 'Well,' said the tombstone-maker, 'did you find it?' 'Oh yes,' I replied, 'and it looks all right. My word, it wanted doing!' 'Yes, I suppose it did,' he said, handing over the half-dollar, and I wasted no time before I was treading the track – for New York.

Some two or three years after, I was working in the vicinity, and took the occasion to visit the village again. There he was in the old place. I had grown a moustache and was dressed in the latest American fashion. He did not recognize me and we exchanged casual greetings. 'I met a fellow up North,' I said, 'who told me he had cut your lawn for half a dollar some time ago.' 'You met him, that gor dam bum? I wish I could meet him!' And he told me all I knew, and more. That woman had never spoken to him since. When her husband died, she had given the order for a tombstone to someone else, and she swore that he had sent a man to ruin her lawn for spite at losing her order. Eventually we adjourned to a near-by saloon and, after I had gotten him into a reasonable mood, I revealed myself and handed him his half-dollar. And then we had a laughing feast. Everybody in the saloon had to be told the joke, and drink at our expense. And when we parted, it was like the parting of two kindred spirits. There is much potency for good in a convivial glass.

However, back in New York, I began to take stock. This life would soon make me a professional bum or hobo. It was during this time I drifted into a large saloon on the East Side by the entrance to Brooklyn Bridge. Unnoticed, as I thought, I was digging into the free lunch with gusto when a voice rapped out:

'Hi, you there, git ter ell outer this!' I went on eating. 'Do you hear, you God-damned bum?' came next. I was conscious that all eyes were on me, and turned round. 'Are you talking to me?' I asked of the head bar-tender. 'I sure am,' he said, 'where's your drink?' 'On that counter,' I replied, coming across to the liquor counter. 'Claim it,' he demanded. "This, I think, is it,' I said, pointing to an almost full schooner. 'Like Hell it is!' roared its owner, 'jest you finger that glass and see heaven.' It was a long counter and I passed down it, looking for a glass that seemed unowned, until I got to the door and shot through, but not before the bar-tender let fly a block of hard wood, which caught me on the back of the head and cut the skin.

Outside, I put my hand to my head and found it bleeding. Going into a near-by drug store, I got the attendant to stick some plaster on it. 'Cut plenty of the hair off," I asked him, 'and make it look a big job with plenty of plaster." He did, and asked ten cents. 'I'll be back in a minute with it," I replied, and going back to the saloon told the bar-tender that the doctor said it was a serious cut and advised me to report it at the police station. It was only a superficial cut. Anyhow I had blood to give away in those days. The upshot of it was, on my promising not to make a case of it and hurt the house, he handed me a quarter-dollar and told me I was good for a free meal till I got a job.

But things had to be altered. So I got signed on as an unpaid cattleman, to work for my passage only, on the *S.S. Cevic* to Liverpool. We got on board, fifteen of us like myself. 'Stiffs' the seven paid men called us. The cattle, about 500 head, and some thousand sheep, were put aboard, and we set off at night for what is yet the finest country in the world. That night I took stock of my mates. We were indeed a polyglot-looking lot of rascals. One man I saw was a Jew, and when he asked me for some tobacco, I gladly acceded to his request. I had heard that grub was not too plentiful on these trips and wanted to make friends with the Hebrew for a purpose. Yes, he could have some tobacco. 'Go on, take some more.' He did, and we smoked on into the night as the lights of the New World receded from our view. 'I say, chum,' I said at last. 'I guess you won't be eating bacon, will you? You might give me your share, if you don't want it, when it is served up to us.' 'Nothin' doin', Bo,'' he replied. 'I'm a Christian this trip.' And he was, as far as eating bacon, or pork, or unkoshered meat went.

The next morning we 'stiffs' were doled out, two each, to assist the paid cattlemen. One Yank, a Southerner, was allocated to a coloured man. There was a row. 'He'd see them in hell before he would work under a nigger.' I smoothed things up by swopping places with him, with my own overseer's consent. The grub was none too plentiful, and one had to be sharp to get one's share. One 'stiff' (a one-eyed boilermaker who had escaped from the Panama Canal contract, where he had signed for a two years job, but, seeing the rest of his mates who had come out with him from Glasgow all gone, dead, with the yellow fever, had made his getaway) accused me, just as we were sitting down to dinner, of stealing more than my share of meat. I knew if I 'crawfished' I would be in for it, would be the butt of the rest's ill humour, so I set about him when he challenged me to fight. Now sheep are subject to a nasty complaint on shipboard, sometimes, and as we progressed towards England more and more showed they had got a distemper, strings of mucous hanging from their nostrils. These sheep were put together in a corral, formed on top of the hatches on a lower deck. In our fight we fell amongst them. What with blood and mucous and sheep dung, we were a pretty sight when we finished, which was only when, by a lucky blow, I closed his one and only peeper, but I had two black eyes and several loose teeth for my packet. The boys turned the hose pipe on us to wash us down before we could turn in with them, and then we found they had eaten our share of grub. besides their own whilst we had been fighting.

We had one 'stiff', an Italian, who had been out in the States only a few weeks, and, not being able to land a job, or homesick, his compatriots had got him aboard. He was seasick and could not work. He simply lay about, rolling his eyes and groaning. Each day there was a minor scrap as to who should have the

Dago's grub, for he could not eat and we had decided, anyhow, if he would not work, he would not get the chance to eat. He could only speak Italian and he couldn't understand that the scrapping each meal time was for his share of the grub. It was his only amusement and he only stopped groaning whilst the scrapping was in progress. We had sighted the Irish coast when he bucked up, and then he made a big commotion, saying he had been robbed of one hundred lire. Two days after we landed, I saw him asleep in daytime, on the steps of the Sailors' Home in Liverpool. I told a passing policeman what I could about him, and the officer got him in touch with the Italian Consul, so I suppose his troubles would soon be ended. The one-eyed Scotsman I took home with me, and saw him fixed up till he got his train next day for the North.

CHAPTER VI

A CANADIAN BARN RAISING

A FEW days afterwards I was myself in Glasgow, working on the new Art Galleries, then on to Edinburgh, then on Lord Overtoun's estate at Dumbarton, then a long trail to London, for I had an idea they couldn't built the Metropolitan Catholic cathedral there without me. Evidently they couldn't, for I got a job there. But London and its late hours were getting me down (the pubs then were opened till 12, or was it 12.30?), and a doctor advised me to seek a country place to pull myself together. So I got to Portland, working in the quarries. Here, one Saturday afternoon, I visited a fair that had been set up. One booth showed a painted picture of a rat, as large as a hare, 'caught in the Liverpool grain warehouses' said the sign. I paid my penny and went in. It was a stuffed animal, half a rabbit and half a rat. 'Do you say that was caught in the Liverpool dock grain sheds?' I asked. 'That's so, Boss.' 'Well,' I said, 'I've spent many days truanting around those same sheds, and saw plenty of rats, but none like that.' 'No, I don't suppose there would be many,' he said, 'but this is one.'

The following weekend I ran over to Langton Maltravers, my parents' birthplace, some thirty miles away. Here I told my uncle of the large rat with a rabbit's head. He laughed. 'Why,' he said, 'it is a cross. Lord Eldon owns most of the land in these parts. For some years he was away and the game-keeping staff was reduced. When he came back to reside in the old hall, he found that the rabbitry was full of these abnormalities, and he had the warrens cleared out and all rats, and rabbits, and half-and-halfers, exterminated.' So possibly the huge rat I paid a penny to see in the Portland fair was one of these. The period of gestation for both rats and rabbits being the same, helped, I suppose, to make the hybrid possible.

On the island I saw, for the first time sheep tethered like goats or horses. There is not much grass land on Portland and the herbage was well chewed down to the ground before the sheep were tethered further on. Their mutton ought to be sweet. However, my summer spent in this healthy spot did me a lot of good. In the long summer evenings, and Saturday afternoons and Sundays, I would be off out to the Bill, fishing. Standing on the flat rocks with my hook baited with a kind of grey water-beetle, I could see the fishes swimming in the water beneath me. It was easy to catch half a dozen rock perch or bream. Sometimes I would build a fire of driftwood and clean the fish and cook them on the embers. In the cavities of the rocks there was always a deposit of salt left after the sun had evaporated the pools, and I dined like a caveman. Sometimes I have seen the innards of the fish, with the portion they breathe with, like a minute silver bladder, inflating and deflating quite a while after I had eaten the fish the apparatus had belonged to.

However, the wanderlust seized me again, and I went north. 1897 found me at Shandon, on the Gareloch, working at a hydro on an extension. The house had belonged to a Napier, a pioneer in marine engine making I believe. It was Queen Victoria's Diamond Jubilee. Huge bonfires were to be started at a given time that night. Our nearest town was a small place called Row.*
Here the whole population were out waiting for the clock to strike the hour at which all the beacons in Britain were to be lit, ten o'clock. I had suffered agonies with an abscess in my gums. At ten minutes to ten I could stand it no longer and entered the inn. Here I gulped clown several glasses of whisky neat. In ten minutes I was fearfully inebriated and saw nothing of the beacon across the lock at Roseneath, except its smouldering

---

* Now spelled Rhu, on the east coast of Gare Loch in Argyle and Bute. It was spelled Row up until the 1920s, but was changed to reflect its Gaelic origins.

embers next morning. But the abscess which had given me a week's agony had burst.

Roseneath, by the way, held one hotel. It is on, I believe, the Marquis of Lorne's estate. Outside, there hung a sign painted by one of the Royal princesses. Four of us masons had hired a boat from a local boatman at so much per week. Of an evening, and weekends, we would pull out on the loch to fish. Three out of four fish we caught were bull-headed things armed with lancet-like spikes, ugly to look at, and nothing on them to eat. I suppose with the cruelty of youth we were hardened. Anyhow, we caught a few of these fish and, sticking corks on their spikes, flung them back into the waters, where they dashed and floundered about on the surface, the corks stopping them from getting beneath, till the gulls swooped down on them. I often wondered if the gulls had indigestion after swallowing (if they did) the corks. This was a healthy spot, described, in their advertisements, as the healthiest spot in the Highlands.

But the road called, and I found myself working at a village, the original, I believe, of Cockpen, of 'The Laird of Cockpen' poem. Here we were engaged on a village hall, given and to be opened by the Duke of Buccleuch, otherwise, I understand, known as the Earl of Dalkeith. Now, some years previous, as a boy, I had been engaged in repairs at the house in Liverpool, 62 Rodney Street, in which the great (at that time) W. E. Gladstone was born. In the cock loft I picked up some shavings, left there when the house was first built, on which the workmen employed on it had written their names. In this mission, or parish hall, the foundation-stone had been hollowed out at the back. The speeches made, a newly-minted coin of every value, from a farthing to a pound, along with copies of current Scottish papers of note, were inserted in the cavity, and the procession filed off leaving old Sandy, the fixing mason, to brick up the back of the cavity. Next morning he was pretty well tiddley. Every half-hour or so, he would get off the scaffold and repair to the pub opposite. The boss began to wonder. It was a new thing to see Sandy with money at that time in the week. Going over to the pub, he made inquiries. 'Was the landlord letting Sandy have whisky on 'strap'?' 'No!' The landlord knew Sandy. 'How was he getting it then?' 'Weel, he's payin' each time for it.' A few more words and it came out. Yes, the landlord's till already had a brand new sovereign and half-sovereign in it. Sandy had burgled the foundation-stone before bricking it up. The affair was kept quiet. The boss retrieved the new coins, pulled out the brickwork and restored them, and kept Sandy to other work till the brickwork had set hard into its mortar, and stopped a few shillings each week from Sandy's pay till he had recouped himself.

About now I fell in love. I must have had it bad, for I wrote:

Does Cynthia love? I do not know,
I only know that in the glow
Of her sweet eyes my thoughts o'erflow
In raptured bliss. An angel's kiss
Would thrill me less, nor sound a chord
So vibrant with my soul's accord.

And if she loves, or loves me not,
One dream I hold, one joy I've got,
For, even if I love in vain,
My sweetest wish, my sweetest pain,
Will, be, to have through Life remain
Her glimpsed soul, through eyes' window-pane.

Her name wasn't Cynthia, but that sounded more euphonious than Maggie. Anyhow, she turned me down, so, shaking the dust of Scotland from my knees, I got back to the Mersey, and in 1902 purchased for five shillings a cattleman's return ticket to Montreal, and had to travel as Walter Tyzack, the name on the ticket. We set sail on the S.S. *Lake Superior*, a dirty little tub with several hundred passengers on board. We were a mixed lot, two or three hundred Italians, some two score Scandinavians, a score of Jews, a party of Doukhobors (a half-mad Christian sect from the wilds of Russia, the men and women dressed alike in sheepskins) and some Britishers, including some forty girls reclaimed from a low life in Edinburgh, Glasgow, Dublin and elsewhere, who were being sent out by the British Girls' Friendly Society to start a new life in Canada, and a contingent of soldiers, Canadian volunteers, the aftermath of the Boer War.

I had sized up my crowd of returning cattlemen and determined to try to better my lot. Getting in touch with the steward, I eventually, for a consideration, got put into a four-berthed cabin already occupied by two passengers. All was now serene. My room mates were two carpenters and we got on well together. Noticing some commotion amongst the Italian contingent on deck when we were some couple of days out, I found they had got one of their compatriots sitting on top of the companion-way leading to their quarters. With pallid complexion and lacklustre eyes he was evidently a sick man. The boatswain had been given some black pills to serve out to any who felt the need for a purge stimulant. He left a couple with the Italians for their sick mate. But he could not, or would not, swallow them. He simply sat there like a dead thing. Over and over again they would open his mouth for the two pills, then jabber and gesticulate. Again he hadn't swallowed them, and one of them would open the poor fellow's mouth and take out the pills again. They actually were making bets for small coins on whether he had swallowed them or not.

At length the doctor was summoned. My experience of ships' doctors has been that, beyond black draughts and purge pills, their services were not much required. No matter what complaint one fancied one had, these medicines would be supplied. The next day, the ship's carpenter was busy boarding up a cabin on the deck for a hospital. The sick man was put into this, a plentiful sousing of disinfectant fluid was gone through, a volunteer called for, and a seaman named Thompson, himself deeply pock-marked, took the job on and was duly locked up with the sick man. He had his accordion with him and was well supplied through a port hole with milk for the invalid and whisky for himself. Now and again his shipmates would hail him to know how he was getting on. He himself was always all right, but his patient 'wouldn't speak', 'wouldn't eat or drink', and then he'd set off in a music-hall song, or a tune on his accordion.

We passed the Island of Anticosti and took the pilot aboard at Father Point at the entrance to the St. Lawrence. A couple of hours' sail and we were at Gros Isle, the quarantine station, after a ten days' trip.* Here the government doctors came aboard in a tug and diagnosed the disease as smallpox. The ship was moored and all hands, captain to cabin boy, crew and passengers, landed on the island. We were the first boat up the St. Lawrence that year and blocks of ice were still floating out to meet the ocean. The island was about a mile across in each direction, the mainland being only faintly discernible on one side. The only trees were a group of very tall pine trees with all their foliage at the top. The few small valleys still held two or three feet of snow. As the crew came off the boat, an emergency crew came aboard in a tug from Quebec. The keys of the cabins, etc., were handed to the newcomers by the last of the crew, at the end of a long pole, and we were in Canada at last.

There were several large sheds on the island to which we were allotted according to nationalities. The Doukhobors had one, the Italians a couple, the rest of the passengers being in another. Whilst the saloon passengers, not many in number, and the girls, and the returning warriors, were housed in a more pretentious place by the landing jetty and fumigating house. Here my ticket as cattleman consigned me to meet and live with them in their hut. But the steward put me at ease again, for a consideration. Next morning we were examined and vaccinated. All our gear was put through a fumigating process, the leather goods coming out of it ruined and as hard as boards.

Every day we had to queue up for something or other. The

---

* Grosse Ille, thirty miles east of Quebec City. Site of an immigration depot which housed any migrants who might have been suspected of carrying infectious diseases.

police had come off from the mainland, and consisted of a sergeant and two men under him. They lived in two small huts, the sergeant's daughter cooking for them. It was then I found my two fellow passengers were stowaways. They had no papers to prove their right to be aboard. I did have my ticket making me Walter Tyzack. When we were all gathered up for inspection, the police hunted through our quarters to see we were all accounted for. But they caught a few boys and men shinning up the tall pine trees to escape going through the inspection. Not afraid of the vaccination and fumigation and compulsory bathing in hot sulphur water. No, they were stowaways. We had about a dozen that trip. However, they were set to work to help the crew, and we settled down to our places.

In those days there was not the surveillance there is today, and graft was rampant. There was so much food allotted each day per head. If the cook could save on that, he did, and the residue which he achieved would find a market, even there. The result of this was that the Italians were woefully robbed of their rations, and kicked up a row. They were of the unskilled worker type, gathered in Italy by some padrone, and shipped, almost like cattle, out to the wild places to work on railway extension work. One or two could speak English and acted as spokesmen for the rest to the Superior Medical Officer, the French Canadian who was the undisputed Chief-in-Command of the island, and to whom they addressed their grievances. From the Italians' point of view, things did not alter very much and there was a tension in the air. However, the next day was some Saint's day and there were evidently some religious scoffers in the Italians' camp. Headed by their chief joker, they paraded around the huts of the others. Their leader, with a crude rope yarn beard hanging to his waist, and a high pyramidical shaped hat of paper, and attended by two acolytes, one carrying a used corn beef tin full of water, the other a ditto full of ashes, would walk a few paces in mock decorum, reading from a paper. He would stop a minute and, taking a crude brush from the can carried by acolyte number one, sprinkle some water around him, then turn to acolyte number two and take from his tin a handful of ashes and sprinkle them on the ground. Then on they wended their way, now and again bursts of laughter greeting some witticism of the leader.

They had visited the shacks, in which lived the other nationalities – all except that of the Doukhobors. These men, or a few of them, stood at their door, no doubt wondering what it was all about. The leader stopped, did his stunt; then proceeded to walk into the Russians' hut. It may have been only a feint, or he may have meant to enter, but the massive-built, but otherwise lamb-like, agriculturists blocked his path. Who struck first I don't know, but soon there were ructions. One burly Russian brought a heavy stick down on an inoffensive-looking Italian, and raised a lump as large as a hen's egg on his forehead. Then the Italians saw red and dashed the door down and entered the place. The crew were hurriedly brought on the scene, the cattlemen were called up as being quasi-sailors, and I was called up, being Walter Tyzack. Our first line of offence was the score or so of returning Canadian soldiers. Led by their senior officer, they lined up with their rifles loaded with ball cartridges. The Chief Doctor made a speech which few of the Italians could understand, but which was translated in his own way by their leader to his compatriots. The leader told the officer it was only a pleasantry they were engaged in, and kept pointing to the egg on the injured man's forehead. He threatened what would happen to the Doukhobors during the night. The troops were called in to fire a volley in the air, to show, I suppose, that their guns were loaded. 'Go on. Shoot us all!' dared the spokesman. However, it dwindled down to a talk on their not getting their fair share of rations, and a heavy downpour of rain sent all hands scrambling to their huts. But the Doukhobors were put in a new hut and guarded that night by a picket.

The officer sent word to Ottawa where Parliament was sitting at the time, and the outcome of the incipient riot was that we were sent off the island three or four days sooner than we should have been. But it was an eerie experience. Several men might be walking, conversing together, when a doctor or policeman would tap one on the shoulder and take him away for detention, on suspicion of being infected. An over-red face was enough. These suspects were kept away from us, and naturally all sorts of stories got round. During my stay I got out my tools and renovated all the tombstones on the island. One, I remember, was a marble obelisk erected to the memory of Irish emigrants who, fleeing from famine and pestilence, came to the New World only to find a grave of typhus fever. Then followed the names of several doctors and priests who had died ministering to them. A sad reminder of the potato famine of 1849 which caused so many people to cross the sea, many to America, many to Liverpool and Glasgow to found the slums, now, but slowly, being pulled down in those two cities. On, then, in a few hours' sail, to reach Quebec and note the imposing falls of Mont Morency to the right, higher than Niagara but with not such a volume of water falling. Then on to Montreal. No work to be got there, so on to Toronto.

Here I succeeded in getting employment in a small yard, when I had spent my last cent. Pay day came and the boss asked what wages I wanted. I was the only one working for him, but I said I wanted the current rate. 'Well,' he said, 'I have no current rate.' 'Well, pay me the top you ever pay.' 'Well, the most I ever paid is twenty cents for men used to my class of work.' It was granite tombstone work. 'That will do,' I said, knowing I was only going to stay there till I'd got enough to make a shift. 'Well, now,' said he, 'I don't reckon to pay you more than a York shilling per hour.' 'And what's a York shilling?' I said. I can't remember now if it was 13 or 15 cents. Anyhow, it was less than I had been getting in England when I left to come to Canada. I thought 'I've struck a snag this time to travel over three thousand miles for less money per hour than I was getting'.

However, in three days' time I demanded the lot and got a job at Guelph (the Queen city) nearer the border of Canada and the USA. The job was at an agricultural college, run by they Canadian government, and the work was an addition to it. Here I boarded with an old lady who claimed to be a great-granddaughter of Bobby Burns. She herself wrote short hymns for her Church periodicals. There was only she and her son, the local blacksmith, with myself and a couple more boarders.

One day I was invited to a 'raising bee' by the son. Always ready for something new, some new experience, I took a day off and went with him. It was a custom in those parts then, when a farmer had lost his barn by fire, for his neighbours to congregate to give him a day's work for nothing to erect the new barn. Hitching up the buggy, we set off to the farmer's homestead, some fifteen miles away. As we neared the place we met others, some with their women folk, and tallied in behind along the dusty unbuilt road. Arrived at the spot, I found some fifty farmers and their sons and helpers. Carpenters had already laid the foundations of rough-hewn beams on a stone-built wall some two feet from the ground. The uprights had been ready morticed and laid numbered near the holes they were to set in. Two men were picked as captains. A coin tossed to see who should have first choice, and alternately we were picked for two teams.

The women stood around, guying some and smiling at others, whilst they handed the food around. And there was some food, I assure you. Roast fowls, beef, custards, cakes and pies, all cold, hot drinks, iced drinks, milk and beer in abundance. But even the man who was pointed out to me as the village sot from the nearest village some five miles away forbore to start working with a cargo of liquor. Then we were called aside by our captain and given our orders, 'you a rope man', 'you a pike man', and so on. The barn was about fifty feet long and thirty feet wide. A whistle was blown and we dashed at it. Surely never men worked so hard for money as we worked that day for the love of the work. It was a real communal effort. The least slip, and the women would laughingly taunt the culprit. 'Greenhorn!' called one hefty farmer's daughter, when one young fellow fell over a rope in his excitement. And my! How he blushed!

Each team had to fix timber uprights and crosspieces,

all ready holed and morticed, together on the ground. Like skeleton gables of houses they looked, when on the ground. The frames would be about twelve or fourteen feet in height from the ground to the eaves, and about sixteen feet to the apex, the wood being about eight inches square of oak. Not a nail was used on this work. They were held together by oak pins driven through the tongue of the mortice. When the end was made up, and the tongues of the uprights laid ready to fall into their places, men were told off to foot each upright. The rest went to the other end and raised the frame as far as they could. Each frame would weigh about two tons. Short poles had been prepared with iron spikes in one end. At each lift, a pole man stuck his pole under the frame and held it like a prop whilst we rested. Then the order came: 'Heave!' and again we bent to it, and the pole man slipped a longer pole under it. And so it went on till it got too high for us to reach, and we all manned the poles. Guy ropes had been fixed to the topmost piece of the work, fore and aft. Then we would get the word to heave again, and, pushing the poles, we would gain a few more inches.

There was no fooling now. Everyone was tense. We had no time to note how the other team was doing at the other end of the building. Should a pole break or slip, the whole thing would come down on us and somebody would sure suffer. At length it was upright. Steady hands guided the tongues of the main uprights into the mortice holes cut for their reception, the rope men pulled an equal weight, the six-inch tongues fell into the greased holes, the ropes made fast, and we looked round, to see the others looking round at us. It was as near as a minute in two hours' work to being a draw.

Then the cheering was started by the women. And we gorged, and told tales, and were introduced, some of us, and smoked. Then, 'All ready?' sang out the captains in about half an hour. 'Aye, ready, sir.' And again we went at it, ding-dong, putting up a side each, and roofing a side each, till, just on dusk, we had finished. But our side was ten minutes slower than the others, who stood off and jeered and chaffed us, till we were glad to climb down, having finished. Then everybody washed. Towels, soap and water, everything, had been put there ready for us by the womenfolk and, after a good tea, boards were laid loosely on the floor, and with fiddle and accordion music the young ones danced by the light of numerous storm and buggy lanterns.

But those with a far journey had to be off. Grudgingly the farmers' daughters left their dancing partners to climb in for home. Many a sly look, a shy look, and a surreptitious kiss was given and taken and I rolled home in a glorious dream of what men could do, if they would. And, mark me, not a word worse than damn, not a vulgar expression, had blurred the proceedings. I had had my share of the beer, but the sweating had taken it off. I felt good. Yes, a Canadian Barn Raising 'Bee' is an inspiration, and gives the lie to those who say men 'will only work for money'. The noblest work in the world has always been done, not for money, but for the happiness that can only come from a feeling of well-doing to others or for others.

I always had an itch for writing, and here, in Guelph, my landlady persuaded me to write a story of *Life on an Emigrant Ship* for the local paper, the *Guelph Herald*. I did. It was my first article, and the editor said, 'Keep on, and some day you may get paid for what you write'. However, my boarding-house mistress set thoughts in my head that have influenced me in many directions.

CHAPTER VII

I AM CONVERTED

A FEW weeks after the 'Bee', I got the wanderlust again and set off to cross the borders into the USA

In Pennsylvania I found myself trying to steal a ride south to where I had heard of a possible job. Waiting with other 'knights of the road' by a wayside station, I jumped for the iron ladder on the side of the box-cars as the train pulled out. I had just got on top and lying down in case of passing under a bridge or through a tunnel, when the brakeman came along. 'Git ter 'ell out er this!' he yelled. I sprang to my feet. Each box-car seemed to have one or two bo's on its root, all preparing to 'git'. But the train was getting up speed. I thought to try suasion. 'I'm only a mason, boss', I said, 'making south to work. Can't you leave me ride a little longer?' 'A mason?' he said. 'Drop down, catch the caboose and I'll be with you when I've booted these bums off.'

I slid down the lantine, found my feet, stood for a while and, as the last car (the caboose) came along, I climbed aboard it. A bunk, a fixed table and at coal stove made up the furniture. I wonder what made the 'Brakey' so good to me, I thought, as I settled down to the cosy atmosphere. 'Perhaps' I thought, 'he has learned my craft in his youth and turned it up for rail work. Perhaps his old dad has been a cutter of stone.'

My soliloquies were cut short by the brakeman's return. 'Well,' he said, as he settled himself in his little seat, 'So you're a mason.'

'Yes,' I essayed. 'And what Lodge do you belong to?' he asked. 'Pittsburgh' I said, 'but of course here in the U.S we call them branches.'

'Branches hell!' he roared. 'Masons' Lodges are Lodges the world over.'

In England we still call our meeting places Lodges, and I began to think there was some mistake being made by one or the other of us. Then I saw the telltale masonic emblem hanging from his watch fob.

'You're only a building mason, and not a freemason,' he shouted. 'You're trying to fly-blow me for a free ride. Git ter 'ell outer this!' And, as I saw his blood was up, I slid through the door, just missing his foot as I dropped astern and came to rest against a tree trunk, after a seemingly endless roll and bump, bump and roll, down the steep railway banks. When I felt sure I had stopped rolling I opened my eyes, felt for wounds or breakages, found them of small account, and lay watching the dawn come up out of the east, and meditating on the littleness of man.

Pittsburgh was my Mecca, but nothing doing, so I hiked it up the Youighenny Valley, to a place called West Newton. Here I started work on a bank. I had taken a turn for religion, and cut out the liquor (not that I ever hurt myself; or anyone else, through it), and read much theological matter. But it got me beat. 'What would Jesus do?' I read. I honestly tried to live a Christian life, and found that, if I lived strictly to the letter of His cardinal principles, 'Do to others as ye would that others should do to you', I should be in a poor house or lunatic asylum very soon. For some months I tried, in word and deed, to do what I imagined Jesus would do. And here and now I can, and do, honestly declare that it is utterly impossible to. live a Christian life under the present Industrial Social System. Bellamy's *Looking Backward* set me thinking.

But a man old enough to be my father, by his conduct and advice at West Newton, opened my eyes to the fool's paradise I was living in. The job, as I said, was a bank, built of stone and brick. A dado of silver dollars, about a foot across them, was carved out of the sandstone. Joking about Mammon one day with the old mason, one Frank Furhmann, the boss, a bullying

Kentuckian, came along and told him to get on with his work. 'Anyhow' he said, 'you are doing that job wrong.' The rest of us knew the old man was quite right in his methods in cutting the stone the way he was doing, to get the desired results. Holding his peace, the mason changed his style of working to suit the boss. 'I wonder you did not lose your temper and tell him off,' I said. 'Ah, no,' he said, 'if I had done that, I would have been as foolish as him.' 'Then you must be a Christian?' I essayed. 'No,' he said, 'I'm a humanitarian, I suppose, in religious matters. As a matter of fact, I'm a Socialist.'

That such patience and forbearance could be shown by a Socialist seemed strange to me, for the foreman had used language that must have cut the old man. I had always been told by the enemies of Socialism that 'all Socialists were atheists' and 'out to rob poor widows of their lifetime's earnings', and so on. And then I remembered that in the early days of Christianity the followers of the new cult were called atheists by those who stood for the worship of the older gods. I was beginning to realize that life should contain more for a man than just working for a living from schooldays till old age made the boss throw him on the scrap-heap. And now the old Socialist went to his tool-box and pulled out several small red-backed books. 'Would you care to read them?' he asked. I found they were five-cent editions of Socialist tracts, issued by Kerr and Co. of Chicago. That night, in my room, I read and re-read them. In conjunction with what I had read in Bellamy's *Looking Backward* they opened my eyes to the fact that I had been wasting my life, or, at any rate, my leisure. But I had denounced Socialism in the past without understanding, or trying to, what the Socialists were after. Hadn't I stoned, as a youth, their speakers at Liverpool street corners, and denounced my own work-mates when, at our union meetings, they had advocated the union's joining up with a Socialist body known as the Independent Labour Party?

In the morning, I told old Frank I was interested but – not converted. For instance, Why this? Why that? How would the people do this? and so on. 'Read on, my boy, and think things out for yourself' he said. And then I realized for the very first time that on politics and religion I had never used my brains to think for myself. At school, at church, I accepted what I was told as Gospel fact. Gospel fact, I felt, could be like any other fact that would not I stand up to logic or reason. At the old man's suggestion, I took up a year's tuition, by correspondence, in the Chicago School of Social Science, the head of which was Professor Walter Thomas Mill, who had been teacher of Political Economy at Wisconsin University, and was discharged for his Socialist doctrines. Was Rockefeller going to donate money to a University whose professor, instead of turning out Republican and Democrat speakers (akin to our Tories and Liberals), was imbuing them with the virus of Socialism? Of course not, so Mill had to be sacked or – no funds from Rockefeller and his ilk. I duly sent my four dollars up, and the lessons came through. Right from the scientific theory of the creation of the earth down to the present era, history was put before the student in an interesting manner. But I hadn't gone far in my studies when I came to a snag. It was the Virgin Birth of Christ that I was impelled to disbelieve in. This seemed a veritable *pons asinorum* to me.* It bucked up against all the things I had been taught as a child. The faith of my fathers had been very real to them, and it had been so to me. But – supposing it were not so sure? Then I began to think back. How did my father know the scriptures were true? His parents and teachers had told him they were true. How did they know? They, too, had been told so. But, studying the early histories of mankind, I found that ages before Christianity came to the earth, men believed priests, or holy men, and worshipped the gods these priests and holy men worshipped. Hence, at one time, my forbears must have broken away from the faith of their fathers and embraced the Cross. They would be looked at askance by their other-god worshipping people. *They* would be atheists to them.

Now I've never met an atheist. That something in all men that

---

* Latin for 'bridge of donkeys', a metaphor for a problem that only be solved by the ablest minds.

strives for happiness, but not at the expense of others, is a real force. It is only the early Jewish idea of a god made in the image of man who can see, therefore has eyes; can hear, therefore has ears; can punish and reward – which many millions of decent citizens cannot subscribe to. But the man who says there is a God, meaning one with human attributes, is, to me, as far off as the one who says there is nothing but the known elements. The man who is impregnable on such matters is the man who says 'I don't know'. Knowledge is logical and scientific, and can be conveyed to others. Belief is not knowledge, though it may lead to knowledge, as Columbus, believing there was land to the West, made belief into knowledge, by going there.

I had always been told men who didn't believe in the Christian God, and the Devil, and Hell, would be men who would kill, rob, or do any unsocial act. Then I began to think of work-mates I knew who were called atheists or agnostics, and I realized they all stood out as the most decent of the men I had met. To cut a long story short, I got over the bridge of asses, and not till then did I truly realize the meaning of being born again. Henceforward I was to live a new life. No longer willing to be humble to so-called superiors, no longer believing in the adage, 'Blessed are the meek', no longer believing in the church hymns, as 'The rich man in his castle, the poor man at his gate, God made them high or lowly, and ordered their estate.' I had a nobler conception of a God than any Christian can have. As a child I couldn't understand how God could love us and yet consign us to hell's torments. Yes, I know some may say the churches mostly don't preach a literal hell now. No, but they did fifty years ago. And the devil was a real monster to us children, and is being so depicted to thousands of children today. As a matter of fact, if the churches ever do let the idea of an after life, of a hell and a devil, go, they will be hard put to it to maintain their idea of an all-wise God for many more generations.

As a child, I couldn't understand why I should worship or believe in a God who was taught me as being more cruel than my father, albeit I had one of the very best of dads. The little incident of the parson in old Graham's kitchen had stayed with me. 'God's will' he had called it, that an innocent child should suffer agonies and die, and break a kindly old father's heart. Such talk is mere fatalism. If a God knows all, He or It or She (Why give God a male sex? Are we males any nobler than the female of our species? Yet even that shows that in the early days of the race women were despised and looked down upon as they are in many parts of the world, and even in England to-day, by depraved mankind) anyhow, if I am destined to live and die a certain way, destined from birth, and He knows, what can I do about it? Nothing.

I had found, as I said before, that, when facing death, as I thought, on the burning steamship, I had no fear of hell. I realize now that hopes of heaven, and fears of hell, are just the wages of conduct as a father may say to his child, 'Be good, here's a toy', 'Be bad, here's a whipping'. Simply a bribe. How ridiculous, when any man who has any pretensions to brains, and of a culture above a beast, knows that it's good to be what is known as 'good' – good for the health, physically and mentally. However, to get back to my studies, I had stuck when at about lesson ten I had been told to treat 'religion' as I would treat any other aspect: study it. It was a struggle. Only those who have been brought up in a devout Christian family and go through that struggle, can realize what it meant to me. I had thought of giving up any further idea of studying social science. But I persisted, and, from that time, some thirty or so years ago, have been a more and more convinced Socialist. To me it is 'religion' enough. And all the rest of my life, since my conversion, since I was mentally born again, has been devoted to teaching, in my leisure, without money and without price, the gospel of Socialism to my fellow-man.

CHAPTER VIII

BEER – AND MURDER

I WAS now a free thinker, instead of a slave thinker as hitherto. In West Newton then I kept to my work, studying more or less each day the lessons as they came through from the correspondence class. West Newton was what is known as a 'dry' town. There was local prohibition in the USA years ago, long before the war made it a national question. Some of us on the job, in fact practically all, were fond of a drink. Titusville, seven or eight miles up the track, was the nearest place which held a saloon, and we felt it a long way to go of a night for one or two drinks, so generally used to make it more, but at last we decided to get a barrel of lager beer delivered each day at the depot, as the railway stations are called there. We rented the basement of the boarding-house at which I lived, rigged up forms and tables, and opened it as a club, for the men only who worked on the job. We were all men from outside districts or 'floaters', and it was more sociable than each man stuck in his own room, at different boarding-houses. So each day I would shoulder the eight-gallon cask at the depot, and serve drinks to the boys.

We found we could sell ourselves beer at about two cents a pint. The natives all kept aloof, and, as we kept the membership to ourselves, it could not be called a 'Speakeasy' or 'blind tiger'. Late one night, however, a knock was heard on the door. The house stood on the outskirts of the town in the midst of weed-grown 'lots', covered with stunted shrub oaks, and desolate enough. I went to the door. It was a stranger to me. A well-dressed, evidently college-bred man of about twenty-five, whose face showed marks of dissipation. It was an arctic night, but in the room, the stove roaring away (I may say coal there was two dollars a ton, carriage extra from the coal pit, which wasn't a 'pit' at all, being in the side of a mountain), all was jollity and merriment, and no man with a heart could have refused him the admittance he asked. And could he have a drink? 'Well, yes.' But we were not supposed to sell him drink. He turned out to be the scapegrace son of the local parson, and was drinking himself to damnation. But as we didn't stock whisky or spirits, the beer could not give him the kick he wanted, and he soon retired. On several later occasions he called on us and proved to be a good enough companion. One night, I had seen the boys off the premises, locked up the bar (I was honorary manager), and had retired to rest about one o'clock. About two, there was a knocking at the front door. Down went the boarding boss, to return to tell me the parson's son was at the door and wished to see me. I dressed and went down, thinking of the dressing-down I'd give him for thinking he was going to get a drink at that hour. But as soon as I saw his face by the light of the candle I carried, I saw there was something in the wind. I'm sorry, chum,' he said, 'but I've called to give you the wire. The Vigilants have had a meeting at Dad's house and have settled to come for you in an hour's time.' 'For me?' I said. 'Why, they can't bother with me. I'm not running a speakeasy.' 'That's so,' he agreed, 'but you'll have to explain that later. They're coming to railroad you out of the town, perhaps tar and feathers. You see,' he continued, 'someone has told Dad you have drink here. Everybody knows you haul a keg of lager from the depot every day, and – well – I'm sorry, but there it is.'

I had a hurried talk to the boarding boss, who advised me and my butty to hit the trail, and, after hurriedly putting our clothes together, and leaving a note for the boys when they came in later, we took the turnpike, a mere cart track, across the hills to a placed called Donora. It was a bit rough, for a blizzard was blowing all the four or five hours we were on the road, and up to our knees in snow, sometimes having to kick a hole into the snow to look for the surface of the road which was entirely obliterated. We made Donora eventually and found a building, the only brick and stone building in the town, being erected. 'Yes,' said the boss, 'I guess I could do with two stone-cutters. You see I have two working for me, but they are on the booze. Do you drink?' 'Only very rarely.' 'Well, if you'll leave the liquor alone till I get this stone front up, you can start and I'll fire those two fellows who've been playing hell with me all summer, working a week and boozing a week, and now, when I should have had the roof on the job, it's only half up, and I've got to keep fires burning to thaw the stones for them when they do come.'

The upshot was my butty Johnny Menges (as he would have his name, though he spelt it Menzies) and I sent a horse sleigh over the mountain for our traps, and walked around the town. It was a one-eyed town, only recently established. The.Steel Trust people had found coal beds and natural gas there, had acquired a vast acreage for a mere song, and, where a year ago was a wilderness, a city was fast springing up. We entered the one and only saloon, to fill up with spirit, for we were damp and cold. Here two men accosted us. They saw we were strangers and wanted to talk. In a few minutes we discovered they were the two stone-cutters whom we had displaced. We drank with them and they with us. 'Are you union men?' they asked. 'Yes,' and we showed them our cards. 'Well, we've been fools, but there it is," they said. 'We don't know of a job within two or three hundred miles from here, and they won't be working in this frost. Ah, well, we'll go across and get the day's pay that's coming to us.' They went over and returned to say the boss would not pay them till pay-day, some three days yet. Would we promise not to start till the boss paid them? Yes, we promised. Would we go with them and tell the boss that? Yes. So off we went. The boss looked daggers at us for sticking up for the men, but paid them off and we made a day of it. Our tools and trunks came over that night, and next morning my mate and I turned out to our work, to be met by the boss: 'Say, you boys,' he said, 'git ter hell outer here. You ain't starting. I bin over to Pittsburgh last night and got two more cutters and I don't want you fellers at all. You don't drink, eh? Git ter hell outer here.' At that moment, two chaps came over from the direction of the depot where a train from Pittsburgh had just pulled in. 'Hello, boys,' he called out to them. 'You've found the burgh all right, eh? Wall, you can start right in.' 'But we've got no tools.' 'No tools? What the hell do you mean by coming to work without tools?' 'We thought we could borrow some till we got our own here,' they said. Then I had a say. Told the boss not to be a damn fool. My butty and I had the tools, there, right on the spot, and – we started.

Now, I would ask the people who denounce drink not to make this episode an excuse for a lecture on 'How men lose their work through booze'. Had these two men been teetotallers, my butty and I would not have got their job. Had we all four been teetotallers, there would not have been jobs for four men. However, this job grubstaked us for the winter. Some days were too severe for a man to be out in it, then the weather would relent and go softer, but freezing all the time.

In Donora, Pa., my butty and I (work being entirely suspended through heavy frost) 'jumped the ties' for a run out of the town on a voyage of exploration. This 'jumping the ties' or 'walking the track' can be quite painful after a few miles until one has limbered up to it. The ties, or sleepers, are deliberately fixed at such a distance apart as to make one pair too short for the human stride, and two of them too wide. The result is one is either small trotting, or doing a kind of spring-jump to take in two ties. Either movement, being out of harmony with the normal step, is destined to irritate the track-walker. One can tell the hobo who's just struck a town after tie walking, by his step, which may take days to wear off and let the victim walk normally again.

However, a few miles west, and we came to a mining village. Many of the people had emigrated from Wales, and, as we entered a dilapidated wooden saloon, I caught some words in the language of the Cymry, from one of the bar idlers. There were about a dozen of them. Men on the night shift, I presumed, at the adjacent pits. Walking up to the farthest end of the long counter, my butty and I called for case whiskies. (Case whisky, I may explain, is imported Scotch or Irish, and more expensive than the rot-gut that many of the States, especially Kentucky, supplied.)

The rest of the company had now got together and were deep in a whispered confabulation with the bartender. Now and again, one or more would steal a furtive and searching look at us. Johnny and I felt there was something in the wind. Presently one of the conspirators stole through the door and the others were passing from hand to hand what seemed like a piece of newspaper.

'Aw drink up and let us gang awa', said my butty.

'No', I replied, 'we'll call another drink and see this thing through'.

The bar-tender left the coterie of whisperers and served us, bestowing on us a long and unnecessarily quizzical look. And now I too got fed up with the secret surveillance we were being subjected to.

We finished our drinks and moved towards the door, when the rest of the company came over from the bar and formed a barrier between us and the exit.

'What's the game, boys?' I asked – when the door was vigorously pushed open and in came the bloke who had surreptitiously stolen away a short time before, followed by a big, hefty man with a jolly grin, who accosted Johnny and me with – 'Well boys, they had you cornered, had they?' Then he turned to the others with, 'It's all right boys, they've got the Biddle brothers up the line, one dead, the other about all in. The woman got plugged a bit too'. Then turning again to us, 'Say, you boys were lucky I came. These chaps would not have let you agone had you tried to, till I arrived. The message has just come through the wires that the search is off. They've got 'em. Drink boys. Boss' (to the bartender) 'fill the boys up'.

And we drank (still case whisky) and laughed again when the rest thawed out and told how one of them had secretly got us 'covered' had we 'attempted to escape'. We had a joyous evening with them, and when we eventually left, they had forgotten the displeasure, which they obviously felt, when the Sheriff told them we were *not* the Biddle brothers. We seemed to have robbed them of the thousand dollars reward offered for the capture of these desperadoes.

It seems that two brothers, about to be arrested in Pittsburgh by a detective named Fitzgerald, shot him to death. Arrested eventually, they were tried, sentenced to the electric chair, and, during their incarceration, were visited by the head jailer's wife, who was interested in their soul's salvation ere they came to 'pass out'. From possibly pure religious fervour for the men's good, she had been struck with the personality of the elder of the boys. So much so that, one night while her husband slept, she stole his keys, let the prisoners out, and, with them, escaped from the jail, commandeered a well-horsed sleigh, and sped through the early dawn into the countryside. They were located, pursued by two other sleighs, manned by armed detectives. One sleigh, on a lonely turnpike road, headed them off, and a fusilade of bullets ended the chase. The jailer's wife had supplied them with guns but they had not hurt any of their pursuers.

Soon afterwards the curtain was rung down, amidst hysterical pilgrimages of erotic females, paying to view the corpses of the two delinquents in a local embalmer's emporium.*

I mentioned just now having heard one of the saloon company talking in Welsh. During our liquoring up I got reminiscent. I had worked on several churches in North Wales and always had a warm spot in my heart for the emotional natives. I found the Welsh miner knew Llandudno, where I had worked, very well. And he also had met a lady friend of mine. Whilst in the North Gwalian† town I had boarded with an old dame whose lovely

---

* Both the Biddle brothers died of their wounds on 1 February 1902.

† Gwalia is an archaic Welsh name for Wales, comparable to Albion for England, especially used in the nineteenth century.

granddaughter assisted her in the home affairs. My youthful susceptible heart had yielded to her charms. But – she would not allow me one little embrace until I had learned to sing a Welsh hymn and attended her to the chapel. How I swatted to learn that hymn! I have forgotten it now but it was set to a tune, Aberystwyth or Andalusia or something like that, and the first line sounded like, 'O thew thew, O thew row hym di baith'. Anyhow, for over a week I struggled with the, to me, foreign words. I made a lot of bloomers at my work that week, for my thoughts waking, working or sleeping, were on my task of winning 'the faithful scholar's' reward. At last I won. I could sing (after a style) the Welsh hymn in the Welsh way.

Alas, a week after my victory, another youth came to reside with us and I was deposed. But I had the satisfaction of seeing another Sassenach going through the ordeal of learning an even harder hymn to claim the victor's kiss. When, some year or two after, I saw outside the Metropolitan Opera House, New York, as I (now an outcast) sauntered by, the name of Jenny Ffoulkes, solo soprano, with the Cardiff Royal Ladies Welsh Choir, as singing there, I wondered if 'twere my Jenny. 'Anyhow', I thought, 'she laughed at my love then, she might laugh at my plight now', and soon forgot. Two years after this I visited old grandmother Ffoulkes at Llandudno, and there I was greeted with an ecstatic kiss by no other than her granddaughter Jenny. 'And where have you been since you left us?' she asked. 'To America," I said. 'So have I', she replied. 'I was with the ladies choir'. 'You were?' I stammered. 'Then it was your name I saw billed outside the Metropolitan Opera House'. 'Why yes, Fred, haven't you heard I am now a professional singer. Why didn't you come and see me when you read my name? At that time I was feeling awful lonely and a friend from the homeland would have cheered me up.'

'But I was on the rocks then and not fit to grace your company', I told her. 'Heavens, Fred, and to think that at that time I was loaded with money and you could have had what you wanted. Poor Fred' – and I was smothered in such a kiss as money cannot buy. But – I am getting sloppy. Let's proceed.

As I say, the job at Donora paid for grub and firing, till at last the spring came, when I got a letter from my old monitor, Fuhrman, to join him down on a job he was foreman of (a millionaire's mansion) at Peapack in New Jersey. This was the most comfortable job I ever worked on in America. In my wanderings in Britain I had found that the churches and mansions were the most cushy jobs, as the work was not scamped and men were given time to make a good job of their work. In the States the wages were about three times as much as at home, but there was little pleasure in working, for it was rush, rush, and rush again. Get away with it. Don't be too precise. Make it suit the eye, and let it go. That must be more or less so under the contract system.

Here, in Peapack, it was what is known as a day-work job, that is, it hadn't been let to the lowest tender, and the men did a fair day's work, and – did it well. 'Give them a good job, Fred', the foreman used to say to me. 'Remember, in the days to come, all these mansions will be taken over by the workers for rest homes and guest houses,' Little did he or I think that by 1917 such would be the case in Russia. I had run up to Buffalo, New York, to see the Exposition.* Entering the Public Park, I observed a large bronze statue of a Red Indian. It was a representation of Red Shirt, an Indian Orator, and recorded one of his last utterances. 'When I am gone, and the warnings of my voice are no longer heard, the avarice and cunning of the White Man will prevail. My heart fails me when I think of my people, so soon to be scattered and forgotten'. Deep in meditation on the truth of his words, I moved on, to come to a marble memorial, centred in a fish aquarium, on which a bronze tablet was fixed, telling that it was erected 'to the memory of Dr. Simpson who introduced the use of anaesthetics for women in childbirth, and, for that, was assailed from practically all the pulpits of America'. Why should this be so? Then I remembered that the curse of God (according to Genesis) was that Eve, for

---

* The Pan-American Exposition, held from 1 May to 2 November 1901.

eating the apple, and all women after her, should suffer pain in childbirth. And wasn't making the process a painless one interfering with the curse of God? Further ruminating that, again according to Genesis, man was, for his punishment, to earn his bread by the sweat of his brow, I wondered why the churches didn't be consistent, and denounce any man who lived on the labour of others, thus escaping the curse of God, or the makers of machinery to lighten, and, I hope, eventually do away with most, if not all, of the hard laborious toil now requisite to produce food, and raiment, and shelter for mankind. And when I think of the oneand-a-half million people in Britain to-day out of work, and crying out for the curse of God (work) to be put upon them, can one wonder if I get cynical when reading of clerical bickerings and evasions?

Whilst in Peapack (a name given to the locality in the days of the red man), I knocked up against the editor of the local paper. He had to make up his local copy for two pages with local news, but it was hard to come by, nothing seemed to happen. The outside pages were supplied by an agency and contained more national, or international, news. The editor, a middle-aged bachelor, took pay mostly in kind, the small local farmers paying their yearly subscription in eggs, butter, etc. So, if a farmer painted his barn, or bought his daughter a bicycle, or was visited by a relative from New York, this would all be news for the Peapack *Exponent*. Thus it was that my Socialist foreman and I, for some months, wrote against each other under *noms de plume*, and each issue would contain some Socialist message. He and I would make up what it was to be. He took the opposite side to me, and I had to flatten him out, many times with his aid. The editor didn't read (only to set up) what we wrote. He was not original himself, and had written himself dry. Hence it was that one time, by mistake, he put my 'reply to an objection' a week before he printed the objection, and nearly gave the show away. We had sent in the objection and the reply the same week.

The farmer I lived with owned about forty-six acres of land, most of it very poor. It had had its best taken out of it years ago, and he could not afford to buy the manure requisite to build it up again. It was a godsend when four of us went to board with him, for then he saw money. Most of the small farmers hardly saw money, as they took their stuff to the village store, and took out goods to the value of the stuff they took in. The storekeeper acted as a collector. When he had a certain quantity of butter, eggs, etc., he sent it into Newark or New York. But he himself was at the mercy of the market in the big towns.

CHAPTER IX

THE SECRET IN THE FOUNDATION STONE

THE job finishing, I spent some months in a marble quarry in New York, and around December had a trip home. In Liverpool, in 1904, I was working in Thornton's Yard,* when the boss sent me to the Liverpool Cathedral site to shape a few stones. I was the first stone-cutter to cut a stone on the job. The present builders, Messrs Morrison, were not on the job at that time. The work was let out, to be contracted for, in two sections, the foundations to the ground level, after which fresh tenders were called for, for the superstructure. This, I fancy, is a business dodge, the people who are having the work done knowing that contractors will cut prices on the first contract, in the hopes of getting the second, being on the ground with their tackle, and from the second contract recoup themselves for any losses on the first. Be that as it may, I was sent to the site. Here I met an old foreman whom I had worked under, on Eccleston church near Chester, for the old Duke of Westminster. He was Mr. Green, the first Clerk of Works on the job, and there till his death. We talked of old times, when two top-hatted men came forward and I sheered off and went on with my work. They were two of the committee men, one, I believe, Sir Frederick Radcliffe.†

'Do you mind if I put a small souvenir', one said 'down into the foundations?'

'Not at all,' replied the clerk.

---

* This is the same yard where Bower's father had found work more than thirty years earlier. See Chapter 2
† Sir Frederick Radcliffe (1861-1953), chair of the committee for building the new Anglican cathedral.

And, gingerly, down the short ladder into the cavity where the old bricklayer, Sam Disley, was laying the blue Staffordshire bricks in a bed of cement and screened granite or limestone chippings, our friend stepped into the hole, some ten feet deep and twelve foot square, which was one of several that were filled with solid brickwork to the ground level, and were to carry the main columns of the cathedral. The other man did the same, then they cleared off, whilst the Clerk of Works, knowing what men are, stood by watching, till a ton of bricks had been built over the place where the money had been inserted.

After he had gone, I thought 'I've as much right to be sentimental as them'. The only thing in the shape of a coin I possessed was a button. But that button had a history. In 1902 I had been in Canada. Walking along Yonge Street, Toronto's main thoroughfare, I saw a black object on the sidewalk. Picking it up, I found it was a button, seemingly stamped out of some hard composition, on which was impressed the words, 'Common Jails of Ontario'. I picked it up. In America most people carry a mascot. A coloured man generally has a rabbit's foot. An Irishman, a small dried potato 'to keep the rheumatics away', he will tell you. So I came by my mascot, and it was the mascot which followed the two gold coins, and now reposes in the cathedral foundations.

That night I had a further idea. As told, I had been converted to Socialism, and was reading Blatchford's paper, the *Clarion*. The issues at that time were very trenchant with articles on 'Free Will', and attacks, or eulogies, on Blatchford's recent book, *God and my Neighbours*. So I hied myself off to a pal of mine with my idea. Here I may diverge.

In my youth at school, there were two exciting periods each year, when lessons were forgotten in a creed feud. Liverpool then, not so much now, was divided into two camps, Orangemen (perfervid Protestants) and Catholics. It was a common sight on St. Patrick's Day, or Orangeman's Day, July 12th, to see real gory battles between the sects. Each believed the only way to get to heaven was to send the other fellow to hell. The civic authorities were glad if these two days passed off each year without murder. And we school children had our battles. Near my school was a Catholic school, and their leader, at that time, was a tall, raw-boned Liverpool-born son of an Irishman. And somehow I was picked for the leader of our school. After school hours we would charge each other with sticks and stones. Sometimes we gave way, sometimes they. What with dodging the police, and the neighbours whose windows we were breaking, it was a great time. But, let that tall leader catch me by myself, and I went through it. Two marks I will carry to the grave, where he cut my head open, or rather the skin that covers it.

It was not till 1912 that the venerable old agitator, Tom Mann, came into the district, organized the workers, got the two factions together, and, with banners of intertwined orange and green, led a band through Liverpool composed of half-and-half Orange-men and Catholics, not playing 'To Hell with the Pope' or 'King William', but the brotherhood songs of the workers. However, to get back to the cathedral affair.

I visited my pal, the long, raw-boned boy, now a man, Jim Larkin, at his house. We who wanted to kill each other in our infantile ignorance had both joined the local Socialist Party and were the best of comrades. He got a piece of tin and compressed a copy each of the *Clarion* and the *Labour Leader* of June 24th, 1904, into it. I wrote the following short hurried note:

'To the Finders, Hail!'
'We, the wage slaves employed on the erection of this cathedral, to be dedicated to the worship of the unemployed Jewish carpenter, hail ye! Within a stone's throw from here, human beings are housed in slums not fit for swine. This message, written on trust-produced paper with trust-produced ink, is to tell ye how we of today are at the mercy of trusts. Building fabrics, clothing, food, fuel, transport, are all in the hands of money-mad, soul-destroying trusts. We can only sell our labour power, as wage slaves, on their terms. The money trusts today own us. In your own day,

you will, thanks to the efforts of past and present agitators for economic freedom, own the trusts. Yours will indeed, compared to ours of to-day, be a happier existence. See to it, therefore, that ye, too, work for the betterment of *all*, and so justify your existence by leaving the world the better for your having lived in it. Thus and thus only shall come about the Kingdom of "God" or "Good" on Earth. Hail, Comrades, and – Farewell.

Yours sincerely,
'A Wage Slave'

This we put with the papers into the case, covered it with another sheet of tin, bent over the ends and edges to make it as air tight as possible, and, next day, I placed it in the foundations of the cathedral between two courses of bricks, and it was duly built in. Some time after, on a Sunday, I was invited to meet one of our national speakers, Philip Snowden, now Lord Snowden, at the house of an ardent old Socialist, Mr. Labouchere, in Grove Street, Liverpool. Snowden had spoken at the Liverpool Institute Hall and his sermon was on 'The Christ that is to be'. Here I met a smart-looking wench who had persuaded a local celebrity, Robert Manson, the 'Lone Scout', to get her invited to meet Philip. By the way, I don't think it was more than a twelvemonth after that first meeting, when she became Mrs., now Lady, Snowden. Here, after supper, Manson, to whom I had confided what I had done, asked me to tell it to Philip, which I did. 'Very good, very good', he said. 'Don't make it public till there is so much weight built on it that it can't very well be removed.'

I took the future Chancellor of the Exchequer's advice, and, along with Old Bob Manson, Jim Larkin and some half a dozen others, we kept the secret for twenty odd years, when it became public property. At its publicity, the building committee didn't like the idea, and essayed to repudiate the ability of anyone being able to do such a thing. Messrs. Morrison, the builders, were appealed to. They couldn't find any old time sheets or records bearing my name as having worked as a mason on the Liverpool Cathedral. But, as I said before, the firm of Morrison's had nothing to do with the job at that time. Messrs. Thornton and Sons were the only builders then on the site. They were engaged in hurriedly running up a few courses of sandstone, to take the foundation stone, which was worked and lettered in Thornton's yard. On June 27th, 1904, I laid the documents in the foundations. June 29th I sailed from Liverpool on the White Star liner *Baltic* on her first trip across the Atlantic, and, on July 19th, 1904, King Edward VII duly did his bit, and laid the foundation stone over my documents.

CHAPTER X

PIERPONT MORGAN AND CARRIE NATION

ON board the *Baltic* we had the great Pierpont Morgan who, at the time, controlled the shipping trust. Seated at the long tables for dinner one day, a steward was handing the grub out. One of the diners asked for a piece of meat. The steward grabbed a piece on his fork and shot it across the table to him.

'Here, mate', I said, 'it's men you are feeding, not pigs.'

He came over to me and whispered: 'It's good enough for them. They only act like pigs.'

'Maybe conditions have made them act like pigs', I said, raising my voice, 'but on the top deck you have a man named Morgan. Does he act like a pig?'

'Well, no', he said, 'he's a gentleman.'

'Yes', I replied, 'but put him down here and let him have to fight for his share and he, too, would act like a pig. The very fact that he has reached the position he now holds shows that he would be the biggest hog of the lot of us, and by the same methods (I'm all right, and to hell with you), that he has reached his pinnacle of success.'

The rest of the passengers, after dinner, were congratulating me on taking the steward down.

'Yes,' I said, 'it was not with the idea of taking the steward down I spoke, but to point a moral. That steward has been made what he is by conditions. He is of the working-class like us, and has to get through his work as quick as possible.'

Before I knew where I was, I had a big crowd around me and was off on a Socialist lecture. One is sure of an audience on a liner. People who wouldn't stay a moment to listen to a street-

ᵣ, on board a ship are often too glad to listen to
ᵣn, to pass the time away. So, every day, I had to
lk. Arrived at New York, and waiting to get our
ᵤᵤᵣ checked by the customs, I found myself divided by
a wooden barricade from the great Morgan. He was an ugly-
looking customer with deep-sunk eyes and shaggy eyebrows.
Heavy jowled and forbidding, though, no doubt, he could be
genial enough to some, he looked anything but the man I, at
any rate, would like for a bosom pal. As I stood by the barrier,
trying to analyse the psychology of the man, one of the steerage
passengers came up to me, a man who had often interrupted
me during the trip and would not put a straight question to me,
saying, on my requesting him to do so, 'I haven't the gift of the
gab like you, or else I could'. This man, then, I had observed
watching me as I was surveying the big fellow. 'Wouldn't you
like to throw a bomb at him?' he said. 'Not at all', I replied.
'We Socialists don't believe in throwing bombs at people. Did
we so believe, it would be the likes of you should receive our
attentions. You, and your likes, belonging to our class, are the
people who, by their votes and actions, make it possible for
Morgan and his ilk to dominate practically the peoples of the
World.' But now I had to leave him, with his god, Morgan, to
see to my baggage.

Safely ashore in New York, I got a job on some fancy
stonework in a millionaire's garden at a place called Locust
Valley, Long Island. The land adjoining belonged to another
millionaire. He had a gardener going around his ground with
a tank strapped to his back, which tank, full of paraffin, he
sprayed through a rubber tube with a perforated nozzle on the
surface of the ground wherever he saw a small puddle of water.
'Nice easy job', I said, as he passed near to where I was working,
but on his side of the fence. 'Waal, yes, I guess the job's all right,
but I could do with a smoke.' 'Aren't you allowed to smoke at
your work?', I asked him. 'Waal, yes, I'm allowed', he said, 'but I
don't want to be a god-darned angel yet.' 'But what's the use of
spraying your side of the fence when the 'skeeters' can lay their

eggs on the surface of the ponds this side, and you can never stop them flying over, when hatched, on to your boss's estate.' 'That's so', he said, 'but don't tell my boss. This is a cushy job, and I don't want to lose it.' 'The eradication of mosquitoes, like the eradication of plagues, of war, and of poverty, is an international job,' I said, but he walked off quickly as I lit my pipe. He was saturated with paraffin and he didn't want to be a god-darned angel. Not yet!

It was now the fourth of July, and as it is kept a holiday, I took advantage of the occasion to run across to Boston to see the house I was born in. Here I spent a few days trying to catch the atmosphere of my early childhood days and to just a little extent I did. It was very like I had pictured it to myself. Coming back, I touched at Providence, Rhode Island, and having several hours to spend ere my boat left, I took a boat to Newport, Rhode Island, where my millionaire friends live. Here I visited the cemetery and observed the beautiful mausoleums some of them have erected over their loved ones. Some of these structures must have cost as much as a good sized town hall to build.

Making my way from the boat, I had encountered a stout, matronly woman, going towards the jetty I had just come from. Behind her, at a safe distance, I noticed a small crowd of youths and men following her. I recognized her at once by her photograph as Carrie Nation,* and I saw her brooch. It was an axe. I had heard of her mania for snatching pipes out of people's mouths as she passed them, and instinctively pulled mine out as I passed her, and held it safe in my hand. I caught her eye. She had seen me. And she smiled. I smiled, too. And so we passed, but I felt a tinge of sorrow for the woman when I thought of the useless fight she was engaged in, in fighting the drink traffic on her lines. When I came up with the crowd, I said: 'That's Carrie, isn't it?' 'That's so, guy', said one of the men. 'She was for holdin' a meetin' in the park, but the cops wouldn't let her,

---

* Carrie Nation, a radical temperance reformer, nearly 6 feet tall, was a formidable enemy of saloons. Between 1900 and 1910 she was arrested some thirty times for her 'hatchetations'.

so she's beatin' it to the boat.'

I eventually returned to Providence, and, still having a short time to spare, I walked around the town a while, when I smelt a smell. It reminded me of England. The good old smell of a fried-fish shop. I entered and had some. Providence seemed to me a part of Lancashire, transplanted across the Atlantic. Thousands of Lancashire weavers and spinners have settled there, and I often caught a few words in the, to me, well-known Lancashire dialect.

I eventually got back to Locust Valley, finished the job, and came back to Providence to work on the court house there. From there, I got back to New York and started working at a marble quarry at a place called Tuckahoe, some fifteen or so miles from New York City. Here I first saw oxen at work drawing wooden sleighs with blocks of marble out of the quarry, into the dressing shops. There seems a touch of cruelty in the way they are yoked together in pairs. If one pulls hard, and the other, through weakness, can't pull so. hard, it stands a chance of being choked, or its head pulled off. Of course this never happens because the weaker animal will pull, if only to 'save its neck'. Instead of 'Gee up!' their attendant calls 'I kar'. The oxen were undoubtedly more useful at this work than horses would have been.

Winter coming on, I was discharged and knew it was not much use looking for work at my trade for a few months. And just then I thought of the farmer I had stayed with at Peapack. He had said he would be glad to have me in the winter to help him cut timber for fence rails and kindling wood, so I went out to him. Here I spent several weeks, lumbering, and he suggested we go out one moonlight night to hunt skunks. Their skins were fetching a good price at that time. Animals the size of large cats, their only means of defence, when cornered, is to squirt a foul-smelling liquid at their opponent. This spent, they can't repeat the attempt for some time, before which they can be shot or clubbed. They burrow like rabbits, or occupy derelict or neglected, rabbit or groundhogs' holes. The latter are about the size of a hare, with a broad snout, hence the cognomen, and they carry two visible short turned up tusks, like outgrowing teeth. Some people eat them, but I found their flesh to taste, and smell, too much of grass to my liking.

However, we went skunk hunting with about two foot of snow on the ground. I carried a pick and spade to dig them out, Joe, the farmer, a gun, whilst Joe's dog, a small terrier, we took with us. We travelled for hours, but beyond smelling them, and seeing their tracks, that night we got nowhere. Next morning I got out of bed and couldn't stand. Joe hitched up his sleigh and went for the doctor some five miles away. He diagnosed my infirmity as rheumatic fever, and, as Joe's wife was 'expecting', and I would be in the way, he ran me to the depot, and I was able to crawl into my diggings back at Tuckahoe. A local doctor was called. 'Yes, it's rheumatic fever all right. How much money have you got?' he asked. 'About eighty dollars', I said. 'Well, you'd better give it to your landlady, for you may get to a stage where your mind will wander in this complaint.' I gave her seventy dollars. After that, the doctor came every day to look at me and charge two dollars.

It was a cheerless old house and had the name of being haunted. The tenants had got it for a ridiculous rent, because it had been empty for some years. It stood in its own grounds, surrounded by tall trees. I might have died for what attention I got from the landlady. A few weeks after I had returned from Peapack, we had some new boarders, a man and his two children, a girl of about ten and a boy about eight. He said his wife had run away from him, but there seemed some mystery about the whole affair. Each day he would go out, to his work, in an office, he said, in New York City. Each night he would return. At the end of the week, he put the landlady off by some excuse.

In the middle of the next week, one evening, I was downstairs playing cards with the landlord. Outside, it was sleeting and hailing to a great tune. The mystery man entered. The landlady had put the two children to bed and he said he would go straight up to his room. He took no meals in the house. Would he not have a warm at the stove first, we asked? No, he'd get right into bed. Next morning, about nine, I was awakened by the children calling the landlady, in alarm. She came up and called to me. I was already dressed, and occupied an adjacent room. 'He's taken poison', she said. I had a medical book, but wasn't sure what poison he took, when I observed an empty bottle on the mantelpiece labelled 'Carbolic Acid'. I got the book. It said plenty of milk was the best to nullify the acid. Whilst the landlady ran down for the milk, he was crawling on his hands and knees on the bed. Fumes were coming from his mouth. A glassy stare came into his eyes, and as I caught him, just as he was falling off the bed, I felt I could have kicked him for leaving the kiddies like this.

He was dead before the landlady came up with the milk, and then, lifting the bottle from the mantelpiece, I saw it rested on a note which read: 'No money, no wife, no friends, I leave this world, a miserable wreck, but may God bless my wife and children.' The children now told the landlady more than she had known before. They had evidently been schooled by their father to keep a quiet tongue. It seemed their parents had fallen out over the father's drinking, and letting his business go smash. So they had parted, their mother took up a stage career, and they were put into a boarding-school. But their father had found out where they were and had kidnapped them and brought them to the sombre house in Tuckahoe.

Armed with these facts, the landlady set off with the children to New York and left them with their mother's parents, after notifying the local police and, of course, the doctor. Soon I was left alone in the house. But not for long. Newspaper reporters came hot foot, for the morning papers printed letters they had received from the suicide, blaming his wife's people for what he was about to do. At the very time he had come into the house, he had the poison in his pocket and had posted letters to each of the prominent New York papers telling them of his intentions. However, off had set the landlady, as I said, leaving me and a couple of half-starved boarhounds in the house. I was in an agony of pain with rheumatic fever which, in the excitement, I had seemed to forget, but which now assailed me with intensity. Getting rid of the interviewers, and bolting the doors front and back, I crawled to the kitchen and lay painfully down on the mat. Right over my head lay the dead man on the floor where I had laid him when he died in my arms. The interior doors were all ajar, and the hungry hounds had the run of the house. I could hear them trapesing up the stairs to sniff at the corpse, then they would lollop down to gaze at me. Between my spasms of pain, I could laugh at the weirdness of it all.

The night came on, the stove had gone out, but I was as helpless as an infant and could not move to light up, when the landlady and her husband, whom she had called for at his work in the city, returned with some undertaker's men, and the body was coffined and taken to New York. Needless to say, I had a relapse and it was some months before I was able to travel to a quarry where I had written to and got a job, some miles out of Philadelphia.

The stone was a bastard limestone of a very hard nature. The curse of industry in America, as in a lesser degree in England, is the multiplicity of trade unions. Trade unions have been for years the only barrier between slavish conditions and the workers. But, as larger and larger combines of capital become possible through the formation of trusts and the beating out, or buying out, of smaller concerns, till we have the Federation of British Industries, so trade unions can only be effective now, to maintain a decent condition of life for the workers, by uniting. The trouble is, there are so many people in authority over them, who prefer to be cocks in a small farmyard, rather than hens in a large one.

At the time I am writing of, two unions fought for their members to control the work in this quarry. Where, in England, we have all stone (whether grit, lime, marble, or granite) masons in one union, in the USA there are unions for a dozen different kinds of stones. Hence, to work in this quarry, where the stone was almost as hard as granite, and, by the granite masons claimed as a granite, and by the limestone masons as a limestone, the members of two unions were employed. There was much friction. Eventually it ended by us all getting the sack, and the job being built of brick. And served us both right as long as we stuck to parochial methods of trade unionism. On one occasion, I had drifted into New York City. The men there had a local union of their own. The National Union did not control it. Should a hundred per cent American mason, or stone-cutter, float into the town and get a job, he was not allowed to work till he had a permit from the local union. Sometimes they would allow him to work on an exchange of cards, from his then acknowledged organization. Sometimes he had to pay a joining fee. But, in any case, he could not start to work whilst one man in the local organization was unemployed. Hence, on the weekly meeting night at Brevoort Hall, would be about fifty to a hundred men who had been given jobs, but had to have the local union's card.

On this occasion I was a suppliant for membership by transfer. We were ushered into an ante-room. Only now and again could we hear the speech-making in the larger hall. Should we, or should we not, be allowed to work in New York, was the question. And now the doors were flung open, like sheep we were shoved into the big hall and told by our herders to put our hands up. Thinking we were voting for our admittance, we did. They were counted and we were dismissed into the side-room again. The vote had gone against us being admitted into the New York organization, by a count of hands. And it was by our own hands. Thus had we been fooled.

One could say a lot of the tyranny, and worse, of trade unionism, in many aspects, in the USA. Just one instance. The master builders of that city had agreements with the men's unions, not to employ any men but members of the local unions. The leaders, or spellbinders, of the unions, on their part, agreed that no members of their unions would work for any firm not in their (the masters') local organization. Hence, if an outside firm tendered for, and got, a contract, they couldn't get men to work for them. It finished up by them handing, sometimes at a loss, the job over to a firm that was entrenched in the local employers' organization. Eventually, only a handful of employers would put prices in, for work to be done. Before this was done, they would meet and decide who was to get the work, by putting in the lowest tender, and what that tender was to be. In large cities in Britain we have, in auction sales, a scheme in operation much like it, called 'the knock'. If there were such a thing possible, as 'honest business', it would not be possible, under the system of chicanery, and underhanded dealing which, more and more, marks the activities of big business to-day. However, I had to move into Philadelphia now and get work in a yard on the banks of the Delaware.

CHAPTER XI

UPTON SINCLAIR AND OTHERS

HERE, I had a bit of fun out of my boarding-house mistress, a rather vain, frivolous piece of goods. She was of the inquisitive type. I felt that my trunk was being rummaged in my absence at work, so set a trap. A song writer of the same name as myself had written a song which was all the go at the time, called 'Because I love you'.* Sitting down, I wrote a letter to myself, as though from a friend, asking me why I was such a fool as to be cutting stone for a living when I could be making pots of money by song writing, and congratulating me on the success of 'Because I love you'. This letter I put on top of my things in my trunk. Next day, on coming home at even from work, there were quite a few heads bobbing from doorways and windows in the street. She had evidently told the street. And, as I opened the door with my latch-key, I could hear my landlady thumping, 'Because I love you', in grand style out of the piano. I duly washed and changed, and entered the dining-room to hear her warbling the same tune. The poor woman was so excited she could hardly serve me my dinner before she began to try to tell me what she knew, without telling me how she knew. 'Didn't I think "Because I love you" a fine tune?' 'Wasn't the words fine?' 'Must not it be a great gift to be able to write such things?' 'Wouldn't I rather write songs than cut stone for a living – if I could?' I hummed and ha'd for a while, but at last I got tired of equivocating, and admitted her into a secret. Without a blush, I said I was the Fred Bower who wrote 'Because I love you'. 'Ah!' she said, 'I knew

* The song was written in the late 1890s in Australia by Frederick R. Bowers.

it. I knew it.' 'You did!' I asked, 'but how?' 'I found a letter on the floor in your room. Perhaps I ought not to have read it, but I only glanced through and I put it into your trunk on top of your things.' 'I must send that trunk to have the lock repaired to-morrow', I said, as I thought of what a lovely pair of liars we were.

However, in a few weeks' time, the frost 'knocked off' all men on outside building work. I was sitting on the banks of the Delaware one evening, adjusting my skates, when a smart-looking pair of lovers passed, skating with crossed arms. 'You will give me your answer to-night, love, won't you?' I caught him saying, as they passed. That put an idea into my mind. I would really write a song and those words should form the theme. In my room, that night, I wrote my first song for the market, and – my last. I crave your indulgence, kind reader, whilst I get it off my chest.

Give me your answer to-night, love,
Give me your answer to-night,
Make me the happiest man on earth,
The future both joyous and bright.

Give me your answer to-night, love,
Give me your answer to-night.
Heaven holds no bliss,
That I would not miss,
If you'd give me your answer to-night,

'Not so bad', I thought, 'for the chorus. But now for the verse?' So I got going again.

Give me your answer to-night, love,
Why put me off for a day?
Long I have waited to ask you,
How can you now say me nay?
My one desire will be to make your

Future both joyous and bright,
So, give me your answer, and let it be 'yes',
Give me your answer to-night.
There was another verse, too.

Soon after this I moved on to Trenton, New Jersey, where we were cutting stone for an addition to Princeton University. Here the masons formed a social club and met one night a week to an orgy of mirth and music. I had shown my wonderful 'song' to a young Italian-American stone-cutter. 'Could he have it?' 'Of course!' And soon I had forgotten it. The next meeting our prize songster began to warble, to the Italian's stringed instrument, a song. It had been handed to me, the chairman, as 'untitled'. And soon the performer was giving my words to a catchy waltz tune. The upshot was, the boys decided it was worth printing. Eventually we sent their charges (fifteen dollars) to a Chicago publishing company, and were rewarded with fifty copies, set to the tune composed by our Italo-Yankee mate, which we distributed amongst ourselves, and heard no more of. It was my first adventure, and last, in song-writing, as I said before; but the joking I had to put up with! It was 'Give me your answer to-night, love', to everything I might say, to which those words could possibly be twisted, to form an answer.

Here, in Trenton, I, of course, became active in the Socialist movement. I may say I had joined the local branch of the movement wherever I was, and became active in street or indoor lectures, or talks, right from the time of my conversion. My first speech was made at a street corner in New York. I remember how strange it seemed to me to be one of three speakers told off to speak each night except Sunday. No outdoor meetings were allowed in the City on Sundays. I had, for some years, taken part in the discussions at my union meetings, so had not much trouble when I got going on the newer, and, to me, more spiritual subject of Socialism. There were mostly always three speakers at each meeting, one Italian, one German, one English-speaking. Sometimes we had too many speakers. And, don't forget, none of us were paid. The spirit of the old Disciples actuated us then, as it does now. To a true Socialist, Socialism, and it alone, can bring the heaven on earth which the Christian prays for on one day in the week, and pitifully helps to retard from coming, the other six days.

One evening, I was speaking at the corner of Seventh Avenue and Twenty-fifth Street. The first speaker was a handsome dark girl, born in New York of Irish parents. She was only fifteen years of age, but how the words of her roused the crowd. She was Miss Flynn, known then as 'Girly Flynn, the girl orator'.* Then, I followed, and after me a nearly blind, white-haired old man, named Peter Burrows. Peter began by saying: 'You've heard the Spring of the movement speaking, you've heard the Summer speaking, now you will hear the Autumn.' He was on the wrong side of seventy years of age then. A venerable-looking, lovable creature, with no asperity in his utterances. Always the spirit of Universal Love actuated his theme. After the meeting he told me some of his history which may not be out of place here.

He never knew his parents. A rough man and woman brought him up. He had no schooling. As a ragged boy, he had sold newspapers on one of the London bridges. Here came to him one day a lady who had alighted from a grand carriage drawn up near by. She handed him a small note and entered her carriage. The note contained a request for him to call on her, and gave her name and address. Wondering what it could be about, he had duly presented himself at the place mentioned, and found it a palatial mansion in the West End. Here, he was ushered into a room by a gorgeous butler. From a further room came sounds of music, and people dancing and laughing. He was in a subdued darkness, but presently a door was opened out of the dancing-room, and immediately closed, whilst a glorious-looking woman in evening dress came to him, and, throwing

* Elizabeth Gurley Flynn (1890-1964), labour leader and feminist, activist for the Industrial Workers of the World (IWW, or the 'Wobblies'), founding member of the American Civil Liberties Union, later joining the US Communist Party in 1936 and becoming its chairwoman in 1961.

her arms round him, took him on her knees and kissed and cried over him. She asked him to call her 'mother'. To the poor outcast it seemed like a dream, or a piece out of a melodrama he'd seen on one of the few occasions he had been able to spare a copper for the cheapest seats of a back-street theatre. She thrust some money into his hands and asked him to rig himself out and expect her again. The next time she visited him, she asked him not to call her 'mother' before any other person. The outcome of it all was that he was introduced into her home as a waif she wished to befriend. But there was another son, a year or two younger than himself, who was never happy unless he was making Peter unhappy with his overbearing and taunting speech and actions. A week of it, and Peter had had enough. The duplicity and mystery of the affair got on his nerves, and he clandestinely disappeared, nor went he back to his old haunts. Eventually, he got converted by the Salvation Army, and was taken by them to America. Here he met a Salvationist lassie whom he married, and together they set up a bookstall outside Fulton's Ferry on Long Island. But Peter, who had long ago taught himself to read, had a passion for reading what he had to sell, and his reading made him a Socialist. And he never heard, or saw, again, the mysterious woman who had begged him, with tears in her eyes, to call her 'mother'.

At Trenton, I joined the local branch of the Socialist Party, known as the Social Democratic Party to distinguish it from the Socialist Labour Party, a party headed by Daniel De Leon, which seemed more doctrinaire than the S.D.P. whose greatest speaker, and candidate for Presidency of the Republic, was Eugene Debs. At the Trenton branch, I found I was the only outdoor speaker they had, so I got plenty of practice. Upton Sinclair was being run under our ticket for an Assemblyman. But he was too busy seeing to the production of his first play, founded on his book, *The Jungle,* to visit us. On the Sunday previous to the day of election, some of us members of the local branch were invited to the local theatre to see the final rehearsal of the play, which was to open in the theatre the next day, the election day. From about five on the Sunday afternoon, till two on the Monday morning, we sat, a handful, in the stalls of the theatre. Sinclair was like a delighted schoolboy. We Socialists hoped the play would be good propaganda for our gospel, but, when it was acted, we found the speech Jurgis, the hero, makes when he is converted to Socialism – in fact all the book's message for Socialism, had been cut out. I told him this after the play. 'Yes', he said, 'no manager would handle it with that in. I had to cut it out.' The main thing the book had done had been to show up the filthy and wretched conditions in which the meat-canning industry was carried on in Chicago. This had caused a great slump in the sale and use of canned meat. The message of the need for social reform hardly touched the masses.

When the play was produced on the Monday in Trenton Theatre, reporters from all the anti-Socialistic papers were there to see what they could find in it to damn it. At one point in the play, the boss slaughterman is staged, trying to force his attentions on the hero's wife, in the hero's absence. This part, the brutal savagery of the lustful boss, was seized on, and next day the papers were howling for the suppression of the play as an 'indecent' play. That night, I walked with Sinclair and his wife to their hotel. 'What do you think of it all?' he asked me. 'Well', I said, 'your book hit the people in the belly. Your play has evidently hit them somewhere else, or the papers are determined to make the people think so.' 'I agree with you, comrade', said Mrs. Sinclair, 'and I've told him so.' 'Well', he said, turning earnestly to me, 'what would you do?' 'I'd try the more to hit them in the brain.'* 'Ah, yes', he replied, 'that's always my motive for writing, but it seems to be always side-tracked.' Some few months after that I saw the play again, this time in Philadelphia. It was a frost. The theatre was not a quarter filled. It had hardly been advertised. At the stage door, after the performance, I spoke to one of the actors, and was informed

---

* In October 1906 Sinclair wrote in *Cosmopolitan Magazine* about *The Triangle*: 'I aimed at the public's heart, and by accident I hit it in the stomach.'

that the play had been boycotted from the very beginning. They could not rent hoardings, or buy newspaper space for advertising. The American money power had killed it. And, perhaps, no genius in the world has had more brutal treatment to put up with than Upton Sinclair, for his fearless exposures of the capitalistic methods of business in the U.S.A.

Whilst working in Trenton, I heard there was an English agitator in the local gaol, so I thought to visit him. He was a philosophical anarchist, an agnostic and the last one who would advocate violence. His name was McQueen, and he hailed from Leeds. He had come out to the States to look for work, which he had got in a printing-house in New York, when a strike broke out in the silk mills at Patterson, New Jersey. He took a run over to address the strikers, on the need for solidarity. Whilst speaking to a large section of the strikers, most of them sons of Italy, he noticed a commotion. A portion of his crowd broke away, stormed a nearby silk works at which some blacklegs were working, and set fire to it. The militia were called out, he was arrested, and was sentenced to an indeterminate period of imprisonment. He had been in gaol three years when I visited him. I rang the bell at the entrance to the gaol, and a warder appeared. Explaining I was a tourist from England, and would like to see Mac, my message was carried to the governor. 'Had I anything about me for the prisoner?' I was asked. 'Just two English papers', I replied. 'Let me see them.' I handed over a copy of the *Clarion* and one of the *Sunday Chronicle* which I had just received from home. In a few minutes the warder returned. 'You can give him this', he said, handing me back the *Clarion*, 'but the governor is keeping the other. Come in.' And the prisoner was brought to me. He was a small-sized, spectacled man, and, I could see, far gone in consumption. After a short conversation about the English movement, etc., he was led away. 'How does he behave himself?' I said to the warder as he was showing me out. 'One of the finest creatures I ever met', he replied. 'If he's an anarchist, I wish all the other guys here were anarchists.' Some six months later, McQueen was discharged and shipped to England, to die in a few months in his home town, Leeds. But I wonder what made the governor bar the *Sunday Chronicle* and not the *Clarion*?

However, having imbibed all the sustenance I could get from Princeton University, the job being finished in other words, I moved on to Cornell University, Ithaca, N.Y., where a fine large hall was being built to honour one of their professors, Godwin Smith. Here I found no Socialist organization, so set about forming one. With the enthusiasm of youth, I wrote a letter to the editor of the local paper, the *Ithaca News*, telling the world of America what I thought of it. It evoked several replies, for and against. The Editor was a professor in the University, and the paper was a side line. He was so fair in letting some of us air our views that I suspected what I since found was true, that he was of the faith, but had to keep his political and social views in the background. The writers of the letters which expressed Socialistic views, I found out and interviewed, and we immediately formed a branch of the American section of the Socialist Party.

There were two bachelor brothers over seventy years of age, who had an apple-growing business outside the town, but whose hobby was the keeping of bees. These men had fought in the American Civil War, and keenly regretted their age wouldn't admit of them lighting in the only war worth fighting in, for many more years. Another man, some fifty-eight years of age, kept a messenger bureau. Another, a tailor, had his own shop in the town. He was a fat, jovial fellow named Schultz, and spoke pidgin English, having been brought up in Germany. A couple of American artisans, and half a dozen college students, were the nucleus of our branch. Taking a room over a shop in the one main street of the city, we opened for business, after spending our spare time for a week in colouring the walls, and painting our title on the windows. Amongst the student-members were two Chinese youths, and I often wonder if they carried the Socialist message, eventually, to their own country. We had great fun at our outdoor meetings. Some of the students were sons of millionaires, and didn't like the way I explained how their fathers had made the millions which made it possible for them to go to college, and, some of them, live a luxurious life. (Some of the older ones lived out, and owned palatial bachelor homes, and had their kept mistresses.) At question times they would fire questions at me in galore, some of them entirely irrelevant. I could generally counter them with humorous jokes and get them into a good humour. In the main, they were a lovable lot of boys. But now and again I would hit the system that made their fathers captains of industry, at the expense of the bottom dog, seemingly too personally severe. At such times, they would break out into their college yell and further speechmaking was impossible for a time. It was no use trying to go on, with four or five hundred lusty voices howling their Alma Mater song: 'By Cayuga's lakes and mountains', so I would join in with them.

Only once I scented danger, when some of them avowed I had attacked 'their' country. Some of the ringleaders seized me and my soap box. 'In the lake!' 'In the lake!' they were crying. It was a very warm evening, and I could swim, so I wasn't minding much, when one of their professors, whom they held high in respect, passed. He sized things up, and gave them a little talk. The result was they set the soap box down in the middle of the tram lines, in the main street, and demanded that I 'got on with the story'. A policeman came up to shift me, as the car could not pass. There were only two cars on the service, running alternate ways, the track, from end to end, being only about two miles long. But the students corralled the policeman, and he had, perforce, to listen to me, also.

On one occasion, the college teams had won all their intercollegiate games on the same day, rowing, cricket, baseball and athletics, I think they were. Then the boys *did* run amok. As the news came through 'Cornell won' this, that, or the other contest, the excitement increased. They soon bought out all the pistols and crackers the stores held. Revolvers, and less dangerous noise-producing weapons, or articles, were used in abundance. As darkness increased, they stole, where they could not buy, all the boxes out of the stores, even second-hand furniture out of the one and only junk shop, were piled in the main street, and set fire to. Expense, to those boys, was of no account. Had they been sons of working-men, they would all have been gaoled. Thinking such thoughts, I entered a saloon and had hardly got served with my lager beer when in trooped a school of them, one behind the other, with their hands on the shoulders of the preceding man, they marched in a snake line. With a whoop they broke loose. Over went tables, marble tops were shattered, drinks scattered, glasses crashed to the floor and out they filed again. I looked at the proprietor. 'That's a mess', I said. 'Why didn't you try to stop them?' 'Not me', he said, 'they can come every week, for me.' And then I learnt he had only to send in his account to the college, and there would come a cheque to pay for the damage, out of a fund that was subscribed to, by each student, for that purpose. 'And', he said, with a wink, 'I may tell you, Mister, I don't lose.'

About that time we stone-cutters decided that our foreman wasn't a nice man to know. He was an Englishman hailing originally from Preston. His way of talking was not calculated to get the best out of men. Cursing and reviling, without cause, each and all of us (though I could make allowance for the poor fellow, for he was being hounded on by the shareholders of the company to produce better results in profits), at length we decided to strike. Of course, I had to be the spokesman. The foreman was very foolish. 'I could go to the devil.' I didn't! I went to the saloon where I had left the men, and reported. Next day not a hammer was heard on the building. The university heads wanted to know 'why!' We were asked. But, 'they were not going to have it said in the future, that the Godwin Smith Hall was built by scab labour'. The foreman was severely talked to, and climbed down. Another foreman was selected from amongst us, we were paid at day's wages for the day we had 'lost', and we finished the building in peace and harmony.

Still, I hadn't had enough college education, so I moved on to Niagara Falls, New York, and got on a Roman Catholic

College, a couple of miles outside the city. I had not been here a couple of weeks when I took a walk across the bridge over Niagara Gorge into Canada. I was accompanied by a younger brother, and a young Cheshire stone-cutter, who had come out to the U.S. a few weeks before. Returning, we had reached the American end of the bridge. The other two passed on into the "town, but I was hailed by the customs people and charged with being an alien trying to enter the country from Canada. I told them I was a born American. But they would not have it. A Bible was produced and I was told to take the oath. I affirmed instead. Then they let me go, especially when I told them I lived at the round house, a stone's throw away, and they could soon settle it by sending some one with me to see. But, had either of the other two been stopped, they might have had a bit of trouble to satisfy the officers that they were not aliens.

This round house was a bit of a puzzle to me. It was of brick and built like a huge chimney. From my window, I could look across the gorge to a chalet, where Captain Webb's widow kept a shop, and sold souvenirs of her husband. He was drowned trying to swim across the rapids, after being the first man to swim the English Channel. Going to and from our boarding-house to the job, we sometimes would cut through a peach orchard for a short cut. The peaches were ripe and we often helped ourselves. Coming through the orchard one evening, we espied a man coming after us. We were loaded with the juicy fruit. The fears of our boyhood came back to us, but I felt it was unmanly to run, especially as the newcomer was calling us not to worry. I waited. He came up. 'Help yourself ', he said. 'Are you the owner?" I asked. 'Yes', he answered, 'and you can take the darn lot. I'm turning the hogs loose in the orchard to-morrow.'

And then he told me why. 'Time was', he said, 'when I would consider myself lucky with such a crop. Now it won't pay me to pick them. By the time I picked them and bought baskets and loaded them into the box cars at the depot for Buffalo or New York, I would be out. Time was when, around about this season, I would be approached by an agent offering me so many cents per basket for my peaches. I would not jump. "I'll let you know in a day or two," I would say. Then, another agent would appear. He might spring another cent or two per basket for them. At last, after a day or two, when I had had several agents come to see me, I would close with the one offering the highest price. But there came a year, a while back, when only one agent came. He offered a ridiculously low price. I said I would wait. But no more agents came, and I got in touch with the one and only man who had visited me. His reply was to the effect that he could only offer me now an even lower price, which I could take or leave. The truth was, the wholesalers had formed a ring. And it was to the ring I had to sell, or see my stuff rot.' 'Why not try other stuff?" I said. 'Apples, or what not?' 'It's just the same. The same ring has got the lot,' he replied.

This gave me a line excuse to get in a Socialist argument against trusts. He began cursing trusts. But I upheld trusts. 'A trust is a good thing if you are inside,' I said. He agreed. 'Then',. I said, 'when the nations owns the trusts, we'll all benefit. In other words the nation must own the trusts, or else the trusts will own the nation.' The night was dark ere I left him, still thinking it over.

Near to the college I was working on the addition to, was an Indian reservation. Sometimes an Indian would short cut past where we worked to get to his hang out. Notices were conspicuously displayed of the penalties incurred by giving the Indians drink. In drink, they were a menace. One old Indian came through the workshop one day and picked on me. Holding his hand out to shake, in a token of friendship, I put my hand out to return it, when he seized it and squeezed it, till I thought he would pulp it. Nor would he let me go. For fully ten minutes he held me, I all the time trying to control my temper as he rattled off in his lingo. The boss had to buy him off with a dime before he quitted his hold of my hand and moved away. 'You should never look at them when they pass', he said. 'Be friendly, and they'll take advantage of it.' But I had shaken hands with an old Indian warrior, one who had fought at Custer's last battle. Not much like the Indians I had read of in Fennimore Cooper's novels of my boyhood's days, and the women anything but the beauties I had seen in illustrations of them. The government gives them so much grain and other gear per year. But they never could take to agriculture, and seemingly, in another generation or two, will have died out.

Near the end of the bridge which crosses the gorge (there are two, but one is for railway purposes only), there is an inclined slope, along which a trolley car runs on a road cut out of the limestone rocks. This road leads to a small place called Waterson, which is the port of embarkation for tourists to or from Canada. There is only one saloon to be seen here. I entered it, one day, the only customer. 'Trade seems slack', I said to the proprietor. 'Yes, nothing doin' now,' he essayed. 'Was there ever much doing around here to justify a saloon?' I asked. 'Oh, this was only a side line,' he vouchsafed. 'There used to be other business'. 'And that was smuggling?' I suggested. 'You've hit it, boss.' 'Diamonds?' I ventured. 'Diamonds? Hell, no! Chinks,' he replied. 'It seems they got a hundred dollars for every Chinaman they got over the river, but that's been dead sometime now. Before I came here.' I drank up, contemplating the changes in the business world. Halfway along this narrow road which runs by the swirling waters of the gorge, and stands about four foot above it, I noticed a tablet of bronze affixed to the rock. Perched some fifty foot above this rock I could see the back of a saloon which I knew fronted on the roadside. The place was called 'the Devil's Hole'. The tablet was erected to the memory of some British soldiers who, in the early Colonial days, had flung themselves over the rocks to death when pursued by Red Indians, rather than suffer torture at the hands of the red men. The tablet recorded the names of several men, and finished up the recording with 'And one other'.

CHAPTER XII

'THE LONE SCOUT'

SOON after this I had word from home that my dad was ill, and I set off for England again. Back in Liverpool, I was initiated into the Pezzer's Society. Robert Manson was the ruling light in a mock secret organization, called the 'Pezzers'. 'Pezzers', I may say, is a corruption of pessimists. As a great honour I was admitted to their annual saturnalia. A night in the depth of winter, when the calendar said there would be no moon, the Pezzers would pick for their orgy. The number of members was restricted to eighteen, and no one could join the order till one died and left a vacancy. I was lucky, they told me, for one of their members had met a frightful death, a short time before I had come amongst them. Hence the vacancy. The idea had emanated in the brain of Robert Manson the 'Lone Scout' of the Liverpool Socialists, who pretended to an absolutely certain knowledge that the 'people' were not worth working for, that life was a horrid dream, and 'Death, the only perfect Life'. Thus Death was to be prayed for, hoped for, in fact the only thing worth dying for. From which the reader will see what a true optimist he was, for Death was the very last thing, the very long last thing, he wanted. He was of too happy a disposition. A nature lover, and countryside worshipper, he spent all his spare time at week-ends in roaming the fields and dales of Lancashire and Cheshire and North Wales.

What a pal he was for pub or palace! What a treat to ramble the countryside with him and hear him reciting the poets or trying out some of his own verses. Not a change of aspect in sky or land but what he could quote a verse or couplet to fit it. How many young zealots he has helped over the *pons asinorum*! How many Socialist pioneers from other lands entertained! How many jokes told o'er the flowing bowl! How uncomplainingly he stretched his lengthy self in my short bunk in my Black Maria caravan. And when at last diabetes brought him low, even then, his sick visitor got more consolation than he could give. How proud he was when he told me how Ethel Anakin, now Lady Snowden, fussed about him when she visited him in the Belmont Home. And when, later on, he was drafted to the institution in which he eventually died, he still, although 74 years of age, refused to believe the gods were going to stop his breath.

On almost my last visit, he was, however, depressed. Returning from a previous visit to him, I had occasion to use the Mersey Railway. Sitting opposite me I observed an old fighter for the cause of the people. With closed eyes, her happy face beaming, I felt it a sacrilege to interrupt her evidently happy thoughts by speaking to her, when she opened her eyes and gazed at me. Feeling I was recognized through our last meeting at a supper in a comrade's house in Rochdale, I at length broke the silence. I knew she had an inclination to Spiritualism, so wasn't surprised to hear from her lips that she had just been communing with her loved ones who had 'passed over'. To turn the subject to something that I could talk about, I told her how I had just left Old Bob Manson's bedside. She was a travelling propagandist, about the only one left, at any rate of her sex, of the early Independent Labour Party days. I told her where Bob lay and she promised to visit him. I felt the old agitator would be delighted.

Later on in the night I sat and wrote a eulogy of Robert, who lay dying, and sent it as a 'letter to the Editor' of a local paper. Next day I received a line from that individual saying he too knew Bob and had often begged him to write his reminiscences. Bob was always 'going to do it', but never did. 'However,' wrote the editor, 'I will hold your communication back for his demise which I know can't be far off now, and put it in as a biographical note.' With his letter was a cheque for a guinea, my first and only payment for my pen work, though somewhere earlier in this book I may have said I have yet to receive pay for such work, this incident having escaped my memory. However, with the cheque I bought a bottle of whisky and visited Bob a day or two later. 'Would he have a drink?'

'No.' 'Wasn't it allowed?' I asked. No! but that didn't matter. I ought to know that he delighted in breaking obnoxious social laws. But I sensed Bob was sad, and I felt awful guilty when he said, 'I wonder who sent that woman to see me?'

'Why, Robert,' I parried, 'I would have thought you would be pleased to have her visit you.'

'Yes, but she came in and said, "Robert, Robert, you'll soon be with So-and-So" (naming her departed kin). "Tell them I am looking forward to being with them!" Who the devil told her I was going to die?' he asked.

I daren't answer for shame, and begged him to have a tot of whisky. Yet I had only done what almost any man would have done, and, within twenty-four hours, my old comrade lay dead and the obituary notice I had written duly appeared.

But I have digressed. On the January night set for the annual 'Razzle' we foregathered by devious routes to a thatched old-time cottage, in an out-of-the-way Cheshire village. Here, a small barrel of beer had been deposited by the local carrier, and, sitting around a huge deal table, loaded with steaming hotpots, the members, bibbed in sackcloth table napkins, decorated with the skull and crossbones, and bedaubed with ashes glued to the rough cloth, the Arch Pezzer (Manson) and his Hereditary 'Wailer', 'Lantern Carrier', 'Limner', and 'Keeper of the Money Bags', with their flamboyant insignia, munched and quaffed midst mirth and melody. The meal ended, long clay churchwardens were passed around, the light put out, and, seated in a semicircle on the stone-flagged kitchen, with a huge fire of logs in the capacious ingled fireplace, the Arch would read out his screed. In it he called on all the devils, in or out of hell, to help us to wipe out the human race as not being fit to grace such a beautiful place as this world could be, only for humanity. Then, like knights of the round table, he would call on 'Sir' this or 'Sir' that, to do summat, say summat, sing summat, but – woe be to the neophyte who hadn't got the hang of it, and started to sing or recite a 'patriotic' thing, or anything not original, or that was not, at least, fifty years old, and told of the glories of ale, or something ghostly or eerie.

When the clock on the wall struck the midnight hour, the lamp would be lit, the last of the ale consumed, and, each crowned with a long hood, we silently trekked into the wild night, to the Arch Chief Pezzer's benediction, to the weather dispensers, for, was it not a glorious night, and 'snowing like hell'? Then, through the night, through the worst lanes, roads and boglands that he could find, our impish Chief led us in single file. Hours might pass and not a word be spoken. Anon, he would stop us to listen to the near-by screech of an owl, then on again. Through quaint old village churchyards, in the midst of a pine wood, where some would lie on the foot-deep layer of dead fir fronds, whilst the Chief would set fire to some mammoth red and blue Bengal lights, giving the whole a wonderfully eerie look. Then on again through the night, to finish up, more dead than alive, in a remote village, where, in a cottage, hot breakfast had been ordered for eighteen at eight.

After which, a bit tidied and cleaned of mud, we would make for the nearest station and get home to our beds. And surely never were our beds so welcome as on these occasions. Most of the members were decent, respectable business men, of Liverpool and its vicinity, and such a night would be their one adventure. And our Arch would chortle with glee if he heard, a week after, that one of the band was down with 'flu or pneumonia through the night's ordeal. On my first night, 'twixt one and two a.m., we met a poor wight, suffering evidently from having had one over the eight. He looked up as he got abreast of our leader, with his satchel slung from his neck. What he must have thought, heaven knows, but he turned tail, forgot he was drunk, or near it, and flew, followed by all the eerie shrieks, groans, and mouth noises we could produce. At home, next day,

I laughed as I thought of my overnight comrades, some solid business men, fathers of grown-up families, having their one glorious night of freedom a year.

But I had been warned that next year I was to write something original – or else!!! I had met Maxim Gorki, the Russian, in New York, that year.* Our 'Hereditary Dirge Wailer' put me much in mind of him. Robert Blatchford and Joseph Burgess had been arguing about 'God and my neighbour' in the *Clarion* for weeks. Bernard Shaw had been asked to decide the question, 'whether it was policy to introduce, at that time, secular questionings of religion into the Socialist Movement'. In his usual say-a-little-mean-a-lot way, Shaw had finished up dressing both the protagonists down, and wound up his article by asking 'Where are we?" The war 'twixt Russia and Japan was on† and Rozhdestvensky, the Russian admiral, had also, around that time, been in evidence, anywhere but where he should have been. I put these facts to enable the reader to grasp what follows. My contribution to the succeeding 'Pezzer's Razzle':

Nebuchadnezzar Josiah Bellew,
Was a prig in his business, a saint in his pew,
The gamut of vices he'd almost run through
By forty.
But now we observe him with reverent mien,
Consorting with parsons, and sometimes – a Dean,
He would frown at a drunk, tell small boys 'not to fight'
– It was naughty.
But the cause of the crusty, curmudgeon's new role,
Was not altogether the fear for his soul,
Or the blast-furnace heat it might get in a hole,
A La Morte,
But the twistings and tweaks, of a robbed constitution

---

* Gorky was sent on a fundraising trip to the USA by the Bolsheviks in 1906.
† The Sino-Japanese war took place between 8 February and 5 September 1905. Bower's chronology is slightly awry here.

Presaged, if not ended, in short, dissolution.
And so, when effect, which so sure follows cause,
By its more prolonged 'membrance
Did bid him to pause,
And, – attempt restitution,
He hied himself off to a Doctor MacGibbs,
Who sounded his wind and examined his ribs,
And strongly advised him to alter his living,
If he wished to be long in the land of the same.
So Nebuchadnezzar Josiah Bellew,
From an arrogant blasé intemperate roue,
Into an orderly citizen grew,
Because he couldn't stand pain.
But twelvemonths to-night, 'tis sad to relate,
He reached Hadlow Road,* and found his train late,
And, having an hour and three-quarters to wait,
He fell, from the paths of virtue.
Poor Nebuchadnezzar Bellew.
He entered the 'Lion'† and called for some wine,
The killing of time his only design,
But, under its influence, he felt quite benign,
And he ordered a stronger potation.
Soon at ease with the rustics, whose wonderment grew,
At his learned remarks, was Josiah Bellew,
And the train, came, and went,
From the Hadlow Road Station,
Leaving him in the midst of a fiery oration.
'Time, gentlemen, please,' brought him back to his senses,
He straightened himself, and adjusted his lenses,
And said, in a manner, quite G. Bernard Shawey,
'I say, Mr. Landlord, pray, tell me, where aw we?'
The landlord explained to the best of his knowledge,
Which of course, wasn't much, he'd been taught in a college,

---

* Hadlow Road railway station on the branch line of the Birkenhead Railway between Hooton and West Kirby, serving the village of Willaston.
† The Old Red Lion pub closed in 1928.

That the path through the woods,
Was the far nearest road,
To the village where Nebuchadnezzar abode.
And so it came out that a year to-night,
Josiah Bellew got a terrible fright,
And resolved,
With more prayers to strengthen his vows,
For he swears he saw devils and spooks in galore,
With imps of fell contour in many a score,
Though his friends tap their foreheads, and say 'it was more
Possibly sheep, perhaps cows'.
But they found him next morning, all covered with mud,
At the edge of the pit, in the midst of the wood,
In a truly deplorable state.
By means of hot blankets, and whisky *ad lib*,
And, after a snooze in his own cosy crib,
They loosened his tongue, overnight far too glib,
And this story he tried to relate.
He'd left the 'Red Lion', two miles at his back,
Though wobbling, had managed to keep to the track,
 Heedless of rain or storm.
When - under the fitful flare of the moon,
A sight met his view, which nigh caused him to swoon,
As Capuchin-hooded, and skull-bedecked,
With never a word as they silently trekked,
And led by a fearsome form,
Came rows and battalions of pixies and gnomes,
Leprechauns, wraithes and elves,
Blindly following their leader as being,
More gruesomely formed than themselves.
A bag from the skin of a bovine corse,
(At least, so it seemed, though it might have been horse),
From the leader's neck hung by an endless thong,
And swung, as he strode along,
And he swore an oath at the rising morn,
At the devil who carried the lantern of horn,

And with a vigour most hellish-born,
Demands of his imps, a song.
And the songs that they sung
Were most gruesomely grue,
Of the gurgling groans of a shipwrecked crew,
Of a spectral Chief in an haunted tower,
They sang in a very high G.
And the hair of Josiah rose higher and higher,
Whilst globules of sweat embattled each spire,
(Though never before was he known to perspire,)
As they laughed in their fiendish glee,
Whilst the pixies and gnomes,
Would advance and retire,
Like Rozhdestvensky at sea.
When – a rift in the clouds, threw his form in relief,
And Bellew thought his stay on this planet was brief,
As a thunderous oath from the Spectral Chief,
Threw all his devils in chase.
Avaunt! Ye Leprechauns, Wraithes and Elves,
There goes a Vampire, none of ourselves,
But one, who in pockets of honest men delves,
A wretched collector of pelf.
Clutch well, that wretched mass of adobe,
Stitch tight around him, the were-wolf's robe,
Cavort him madly around the Globe,
And drop him in Allerton Delph.
With desperate effort, he tried to turn tail,
Whilst the wiltering, whimpering Banshee's wail,
Like the Storm Demon's laugh in an Ocean gale
Helped cause him to quicken his pace,
Whiles the glistening gleam of a ghastly glint,
From the Leprechaun's nostrils conveyed him a hint
That soon, in his blood, it might wallow.
When, right in a pit, where the sedge-grass grew,
Floundered poor Nebuchadnezzar Bellew
Up to his neck, yet he dare not Holloa,

For fear a more diresome fate might follow.
Around the pit, a doleful dirge,
Where impious oath and prayer did merge,
Then chanted, in sepulchral tones,
A blight on the wretched man's hopes of heaven,
Murrains, and diseases, seven times seven,
They prayed might soon visit his bones.
From a cleft in his bag, the Chief quickly drew,
A collection of spirits yclept Roderick Dhu,
Which, waving aloft to his satellites' view,
He drank 'to Josiah's damnation'.
A parchment from his monkish garb,
He next produced and with phosphorous barb,
Repeatedly tried to ignite
And failed.
Across his body a lightning streak,
Ending in flame and a noisome reek,
He made,
And at each failure his demons groaned,
Whilst the Gorki-featured wailer moaned,
And the Banshee wildly wailed,
And many a curse injected speech,
Was heard 'midst the general howl and screech,
And Nebuchadnezzar prayed God he might reach,
His home.
Never again, he said o'er and o'er,
Of the Lion Hotel would he enter the door,
Never again would he roam.
At length, he succeeds and a pinnacled mass
Like a miniature Hell, that, concealed in the grass,
Stood erected,
He inspired, and a glimmer of ghastly hue,
An increasing circle of vapoury blue,
Dispels the gloom, and their outlines threw,
To Gargantuan proportions.
He remembers no more,

But, covered with slutch,
And grasped in his hand in a death-like clutch,
Was a blackened and charred piece of paper,
'Twas written in red, which might have been blood,
Two words and two only were quite understood,
'Dear Bob'.
And they tell in those parts of Josiah Bellew,
How, alone, unaided, and singly he slew
The Devil and all his rampageous crew
In the woods.
When pressed for their proof they will slily retort,
'Well, Bob, you know, for Robert's the short,
And of 'Robert the Devil' you've heard by report,
So I guess I've delivered the goods.

CHAPTER XIII

JIM LARKIN

IN this year, 1906, the Parliamentary elections were on and the Liverpool West Toxteth branch of the Labour Party was running a Parliamentary candidate against a man named Houston, a millionaire ship-owner, who, in spite of his reputed seven millions, lived in the Channel Islands and thus escaped income tax. No man, or party, was more lavish in their bombastic patriotism than were our opponents. Our candidate was known to be a Catholic, and believed to be a Socialist, and perhaps the worst man we could have selected for such a bigoted Orange district.* I acted under my boyhood's enemy, Jim Larkin, as assistant election agent. A day or two previous to the election, Jim had a great idea. The Boer War three or four years ago had not been forgotten. When that was over, the workers in England were beginning to ask what it was all about, and, where did they come in. To stop this querying from leading to knowledge, Joseph Chamberlain introduced his scheme of Tariff Reform, as a red herring. It acted. It drew the workers away into two camps, for and against tariffs. Free Trade or Protection fooled the workers, and they were led up the garden of political inconsequence again. But Chinese had been imported into South Africa, to bring down the wages of white workers. The workers were told Africa was not a white man's country. They could fight in it, and die in it, but couldn't stand the climate to

---

*   The labour candidate was James Sexton, leader of the National Union of Dock Labourers in Liverpool, later to be elected as MP for St Helen's. Sexton was a moderate who became the enemy of the radical Larkin, which perhaps explains why Bower does not name him, and why he sarcastically remarks that Sexton was 'believed to be a socialist'.

work in it, and so on.

This Houston, then, had voted for the Chinese labour, so
'Chinese Slavery' was the battle-cry against him. Larkin had
got a glass-sided hearse, and several cabs. The Labour-women
had worked all the hours they could spare from home ties, in
making loose-fitting, overall pants and coats, out of a cheap
yellow cloth material. I had cadged a dozen picks and a dozen
shovels from a friendly contractor in the neighbourhood. Some
fifty members of the Dockers' Union, who were unemployed,
were garbed *a la* Chinese. Headed by a brass band, playing the
Dead March in Saul, the pseudo Chinamen trailed with their
shouldered implements, behind the hearse, in which a coffin-
shaped box, draped with the Union Jack, reposed. And so, on
the election eve, the cortege wended its way through the main
streets. of the constituency. It was supposed to represent the
burial of Freedom. To make it more realistic, Larkin had got
hold of some decoction which he got the men to put on their
faces and hands, which gave them a yellow countenance, and he
himself had made them pigtails, out of oakum, the which they
had pinned to their caps.

At last they returned from the tour, and were paid off for their
three hours' work, at trade union pay. But, when they came to
be paid, the fifty had grown to a hundred. Some had only the
pigtail to show, some a pick, or shovel, some a coat, or a pair
of pants. They had shared the gear with their mates, and, as no
names had been taken, Jim couldn't tell whom he had engaged,
and whom he hadn't. It was twelve o'clock at night when I left
them barging, and went home to bed. And there were some two
or three score of men who didn't dare to go to the docks and
look for a job unloading Houston's boats, for a week after, when
the yellow dye had worn off their faces.

There had been a dockers' strike just before this, and Larkin,
who was a foreman for the loading and unloading of boats, came
out on strike with the men. He was the only foreman along the
line of docks to come out in sympathy with the men. Of course,
he could not expect to get work at the docks any more. The

Dockers' Union, therefore, offered him a job as a paid organizer. He accepted and was sent to Ireland to try to form branches of the union there. He succeeded in Dublin, then went to Belfast. Hitherto, the men in both ports were at daggers drawn. When the Dublin men struck for better conditions, the boats were sent on to Belfast, to be cleared and reloaded by the Orange dockers of Belfast. When the Belfast workers kicked over the traces, the boats were sent to Dublin to be worked by the Dublin Roman Catholic dockers. The Irish bosses never let their own creeds interfere with their solidarity where profits were concerned, but kept the idiotic idea of hatred on religious grounds to the fore, to keep their workers apart. Larkin stopped all that.

He invited me over to give a talk to his members in Belfast. There I saw a band composed of Orangemen and Catholics marching together, units all in one workers' army. As Jim and I lay abed together, that week, we had many things to talk of. It all seemed so wonderful from the days when, as school children, we pined for each other's gore. In the boarding-house one day, the white-haired, motherly landlady said to me: 'Are you a Protestant?' 'Yes,' I said, 'I was brought up so.' 'Well, do you know,' she went on, 'a month ago, I would have cut your throat before I would have let you enter my house. But Mr. Larkin has changed all that'. 'Ah, mother!' I said, 'I, too, was foolish, years ago, and at that time felt like you did a month ago. The only difference is that my eyes were opened to the nonsense of it all before yours were'.

The outcome of Larkin's activities in Ireland was the formation of the Irish Transport Workers' Union, along with the help of that great-souled Irishman, Jim Connolly. I may touch on Ireland later. Anyhow, in 1908, other things were happening in the world. There was industrial trouble in Spain. The population in that country were most illiterate. The only schooling the children got was in the clerical-controlled schools. A fairly rich Spaniard, Francisco Ferrer, had financed and set up schools, where the children of the workers were taught to

read and write. The workers in Barcelona had gone on strike.*
The clergy, dominant, in fact all-powerful, in Spain, tried to
inculpate Ferrer in the dispute. He was arrested, but, after some
time, finding they could not prove any connection between the
Barcelona riots and his teachings, the courts had to let him go.
In a few days, however, martial law was proclaimed.

But, in the interim, Ferrer had come on a visit to Liverpool.
Here he was advised to remain. The local Socialists gave him
a reception dinner. I was pleased to follow the gallant fighter
for education at the speech-making. But he persisted in going
back to Spain. And only a week after we had foregathered in
Liverpool, he was murdered by the Spanish Crown at the clerics'
behest. Shot like a beast by a platoon of soldiers.† If anyone
wants to know why things have happened in Spain since, why
Alfonzo dare not show his head in the country, why the clerics
are having a rough time, they may know that the echoes of that
platoon's rifles outside the walls of Montjuich gaol have not yet
ceased to reverberate.

Over in Ireland, Larkin and Connolly were enthusing
the workers with a belief in, and a knowledge of their own
importance as a class. I had run over to Dublin when they had
a big strike on.‡ Before we left their headquarters, Liberty Hall,
to speak off a wagonette opposite, I was introduced to a fine
set-up, distinguished-looking man, who said he had just come
to see for himself what the Labour Movement stood for. He was
Captain White, son of the general who had held out so bravely
at Ladysmith during the Boer War. Talking together, we reached
the huge crowd of strikers and their sympathizers awaiting the
speech-making. He was for staying on the verge of the crowd,
but, pushing him in front of me, and telling him he would
be able to hear better on the wagon, I got him to the rostrum

---

* This was the so-called 'Tragic Week' of 25 July to 2 August 1909. Bower's
chronology is again slightly awry.
† Ferrer was executed on 13 October 1909.
‡ This strike and the subsequent events described by Bower was the Dublin
Lock-out of 1913. He has plainly got the chronology very wrong here,
perhaps conflating the 1913 events with an earlier dispute.

and he mounted. The meeting started, and, after Connolly had called on me, I got going. 'And now,' I said, as I drew to a close, 'I have the great pleasure of calling upon the son of the Hero of Ladysmith to address you.' 'But I've never spoken to a meeting like this before,' he said to me, as I sat down. 'Why did you announce me to speak? I never came here for that.' 'It's all right, my friend, say what you feel is true, and, anyhow, they're clapping their hands and waiting for you.'

So up he got, explained the position, made an earnest speech, and, from that day, became a thorn in the side of the class from which he had sprung. Batoned and gaoled for his work for freedom, he still carries on, doing his bit to justify his existence.

At one time the Irish Transport Workers' Funds were almost extinct, and, to help to carry on, it was thought a good plan to hand any strikers' children (whose parents agreed) to foster-homes in England. With their youngsters cared for, the men could take another pull at their belts and carry on. Hence, I was asked to meet in Liverpool a party of strikers' children, and escort them to homes where they had been offered hospitality. The time was five o'clock in the morning, when I waited at the Liverpool landing-stage, as the *Carlow* nosed alongside. Detective Inspector McCoy came up to me. We knew each other. 'Hello,' he said. 'What brings you down here so early?' 'The same business as what brings you, I expect, Inspector,' I replied. 'I hope there will be no trouble.' 'There won't be any, if I can help it,' he promised. The gangway was let down, and I went aboard to meet Miss Neale who had charge of the bairns, pinched and ill-clad, most of them barefooted. I set off to board the ferry-boat which was to take us over the Mersey to a beautiful house in Cheshire, the occupant of which had promised to act as host for the children till they had all been fixed up in their respective destinations, when a priest stopped me. 'Where are you going with the children?' he asked. I told him. 'Have you their parents' permission?' 'Not on me,' I replied, 'but it has been given.' 'Then I must give you in charge,' he said, and called a policeman. I explained to the officer. The detective inspector could vouch that I was known to him. Eventually we were corralled into a customs shed around a fire, and the children were regaled with cakes and hot tea. Another priest, a canon, had now appeared and began asking the scared mites what church they went to, had they attended Mass, and so on. The priests soon had the poor children crying. I said, 'If you please, you might leave the children alone, they were quite comfortable before you interfered'. Other things were said, but Miss Neale soothed the youngsters, and we waited.

In about a couple of hours, Inspector McCoy came back, to report the police had got in touch with the Lord Mayor of Dublin. 'He had the written consent of all the parents in his hands,' he said. So we were allowed to pass on. 'Now,' I said to the two priests, 'they are in my charge and you will have to stop annoying them, or else I shall call a policeman.' 'But may we go with you?' one said. 'I cannot stop you,' I replied, 'the, ferry-boat doesn't belong to me.' A Press photographer had come aboard and asked me would I mind posing the children. 'Not at all,' I replied. 'It may evoke sympathy with the plight of their parents, amongst the unthinking general public.' I stood at the end of the line and just as the camera was going to click, the priest stood in the centre, and bless me, if the picture didn't appear with me cut off and an article stating 'our picture shows some of the strikers' Children being taken to palatial foster-homes in the charge of Father Walsh of Liverpool'. The employers in Ireland were using the clergy to beat the workers into submission, by spreading the lie about that the children were going to be turned into Protestants. It was some three months afterwards when I escorted the children back. Now, bonnie and strong and well-dressed their own mothers hardly knew them. It surely would be a red-letter period in those kiddies' lives.

CHAPTER XIV

STRIKES AND TOM MANN

ABOUT 1907 I was selected to try to break up the Liberal and Tory political gangsters who for years had sham-fought each other in Liverpool to 'represent the interests' of the 'paupers' and the 'poor rate' payers. Whichever clique ruled had the giving of contracts for workhouse supplies and building improvements, also more or less safe and cushy jobs. My election expenses practically all came from the really precious pennies of the workers. We had one motor-car promised us for the day of election to bring aged and feeble voters to the poll. An official of the Dockers' Union however had a friend who owned one or two horse-drawn equipages and I was to meet him and be introduced to a Mr. McGuffie of Woolton to beg a carriage for our use on the day when 'Jack's as good as his master'.

Meeting that gentleman at an old-time mansion he owned on the city outskirts, I was hospitably entertained and stated my desire.* Certainly I could have a car. It would be at my committee room at eight on the morning of the election. Highly elated I drank his health and departed. The day came and the car was there. But – it was an Irish jaunting car and the majority of the voters in 'my constituency' were mainly of the Protestant, if not bigoted Orange, section of the community. I sensed trouble when the rumour went round that we of the Labour and Socialist Party were Papists in disguise. 'Take the damn thing away from my door,' said the first dozen old voters we tried to induce to mount our quaint (in England) chariot.

---

* This was Woolton Hall, described in 1911 as a 'Hydropathic Hotel', proprietor Andrew McGuffie. It is now called the Pub in the Park.

Our driver was getting pretty well 'heeled', stopping whenever he could outside a pub to 'have a wee one', when at last one brave old dame said she would be our first customer. She was -and our last. After much heaving and pulling we had hoisted her sixteen stone aboard to the unbounded merriment of her neighbours. A crack of the whip and the Jehu was in his element. He had justified his boss sending the 'car'. But he also justified the saying 'There's danger in drink', for in swerving around corners he took too sharp a curve, and our capture, clinging like mad to the crazy seat and calling upon the saints to preserve her, was shaken from her moorings and flopped into the road. A crowd of noisy urchins of all ages gathered round. She was 'dead', she was dying, and soon -She had been murdered. Such were the rumours spread around. However, soothed and solaced, but limping badly, she spat in the driver's face and returned to her home, while my agent sent the man about his business.

Some months after this I was recovering from a bad time after a bout of rheumatic fever. I was in a bed in the Liverpool Southern Hospital. Listlessly I lay whilst the nurses saw to a new patient they were putting in the bed next to me. A plump rosy-faced man with his head encased in bandages lay facing me. He seemed to recognize me. Pulling the bandage a bit to one side to let his voice come through, he piped out 'Hello, Mr. Bower'. I could never have placed him in his mummy-like uniform when he essayed to gurgle again. 'Don't you know me?' he asked, then added, 'I drove the jantin car fer you at the 'lection.' I had just escaped from the threshold of death, and was too feeble to say or feel what I might have done on another occasion and turned my back to him. Later he told me how setting out he had encountered a couple of Irishmen who had plied him with drink in return, for a ride in their native chariot. After that he was dogged by our opponents' emissaries determined to put his services out of action by making him drunk. Later in the day a sympathizer led the horse and car home, and he himself got sacked. But he had lost us some votes. However since then our movement has practically wiped out the opposition.

Some time after this I was visited by Jim Larkin in Liverpool.* 'Write me something for my paper, the *Irish Worker*,' he commanded me. So I got my writing tackle and wrote an 'Open Letter to British Soldiers', and it duly appeared. As this led to quite a commotion at the time in this country, and was translated, I've been told, into half a dozen other languages, it may not be amiss if I insert it. In the prosecutions that followed on its publication, it was quoted in the courts, and printed verbatim in most of the papers of the day. However, for the interest it might give to a newer generation, here it is:

OPEN LETTER TO BRITISH SOLDIERS

Men! Comrades! Brothers!

YOU are in the army.

So are WE. YOU, in the army of Destruction. WE in the Industrial, or Army of Construction.

WE work at mine, mill, forge, factory, or dock, producing and transporting all the goods, clothing, and stuffs which makes it possible for people to live.

YOU ARE WORKING MEN'S SONS.

When WE go on Strike to better OUR lot, which is the lot also of YOUR FATHERS, MOTHERS, BROTHERS, and SISTERS, YOU are called upon by your officers to MURDER US.

Don't do it!

You know how it happens. Always has happened.

WE stand out as long as we can. Then one of our (and your) irresponsible Brothers, goaded by the sight and thought of his and his loved ones' misery and hunger, commits a crime on property. Immediately YOU are ordered to MURDER US, as YOU did at Mitchellstown, at Featherstone, at Belfast.

Don't YOU know, that when YOU are out of the colours, and become a 'Civvy' again, that YOU, like US, may be on Strike, and YOU, like us, be liable to be MURDERED by other soldiers.

---

* Again the chronology is suspect here. 'Some time after this' means a jump from 1907 to the 1911 Liverpool General Transport Strike.

Boys, DON'T DO IT!

'THOU SHALT NOT KILL' says the Book.

DON'T FORGET THAT!

It does not say, 'unless you have a uniform on'.

No! MURDER IS MURDER, whether committed in the heat of anger, on one who has wronged a loved one, or

by pipe-clayed Tommies with a. rifle.

BOYS, DON'T DO IT!

ACT THE MAN! ACT THE BROTHER! ACT THE HUMAN BEING!

Property can be replaced! Human life, never!

The Idle Rich Class, who own and order you about, own and order us about also. They, and their friends, own the land and means of life, of Britain.

YOU DON'T! WE DON'T.

When WE kick, they order YOU to MURDER us.

When YOU kick, YOU get court-martialled and cells.

YOUR fight is OUR fight. Instead of fighting AGAINST each other, WE should be fighting WITH each other.

Out of OUR loins, OUR lives, OUR homes, YOU came.

Don't disgrace YOUR PARENTS, YOUR CLASS, by being the willing tools any longer of the MASTER CLASS.

YOU, like us, are of the SLAVE CLASS. When WE rise YOU rise; when WE fall, even by your bullets, YE fall also.

England with its fertile valleys and dells, its mineral resources, its sea harvests, is the heritage of ages to us.

YOU no doubt joined the army out of poverty.

WE work long hours, for small wages, at hard work, because of OUR poverty. And both YOUR poverty, and OURS, arises from the fact that Britain, with its resources, belongs to only a few people. These few, owning Britain, own OUR jobs. Owning OUR jobs, they own OUR very LIVES. Comrades, have WE called in vain? Think things out and refuse any longer to MURDER YOUR KINDRED. Help us to win back BRITAIN for the BRITISH, and the WORLD for the WORKERS!

Only a month or so after this, a big strike took place in Liverpool. The strikers, or their friends, got hold of this letter, and distributed copies of it in a leaflet form. Unknown to me, a newspaper just started, called *The Syndicalist*, got hold of a copy, and printed it in its first issue. The outcome of it was that the editor of that paper (Guy Bowman), the printers (two brothers named Buck), Tom Mann (the Secretary), and a young zealot named Fred Crowsley (who got hold of one of the leaflets, and thought so much of it that, at his own expense, he had some hundreds of it reprinted, which he himself distributed), all got gaoled, from one to six months.* I had offered to give myself up, but Tom Mann would not hear of it. 'It will only mean one more victim for them,' he said, 'so why do it?'

Over and over again, Larkin, in his paper (the first to print it), asked to be arrested, but the authorities left him alone. I fancy, at the end, they were sorry they ever touched it. About this time, Jim came over to Liverpool to bury his mother. Never had a mother such a worshipping son. As we came from the cemetery we sat together. Not a word was spoken, but I sensed his hurt. Leaving the mourners, we went to the centre of the town, where a Labour meeting was in force. Espying Jim, the crowd called on him to speak. I tried to draw him away; but, no. The boys wanted him, and on the wagon he got, and soon his passionate utterances thrilled the crowd. Perhaps, at the instant, I was the only one in the crowd who knew of his recent ordeal, for Jim was never one to parade his domestic woes to anyone, when a hooligan in the crowd shouted out in derision a vile epithet. Springing from the wagon on to the heads of the crowd, and then cleaving his way through them, he got to the wretched interrupter, and I shudder to think what might have happened, had not two or three Labour women been by, who, throwing their arms around Jim, gave the miscreant a chance to escape, of which he availed himself.

On two different occasions Jim has been gaoled in Ireland, and twice I have visited him in gaol. But he never quailed. He felt

* The trials took place between February and June 1912.

he was doing right and went on with his work as soon as he was freed. In Liverpool, some of the most advanced Socialists had formed a small club known as the International Club. We were only some twenty-five or so, mostly of different nationalities. My old college professor from the Chicago School of Social Science was on a tour of England, and we took a hall, and, with the co-operation of the local Labour Party, engaged the professor to speak on 'Internationalism'.* We arranged to, as far as possible, have all the persons on the platform, men born in different countries.

One of our members, Lee Foo, was a pleasant-faced Chinaman, who acted as an interpreter at the local police courts, when any of his countrymen were in the hands of the police. Then we had a fine upstanding character named Portet, who had been charged by Ferrer, on his visit to England a week before his death, to carry on the educational work in Spain, if anything should happen, which, as you have read, did. Lipschinski, the artist, had only come amongst us to get subjects. He was a wonderful portrait painter. A painting by him of the Liverpool University professors adorns the walls of that building, at the present moment. Then we had Ali Hassan, an Egyptian interpreter, employed at a large Liverpool café, Sphinx-like in look, action or inaction, and speech. But, when he did speak, it was worth listening to. A Hindoo had been acquired from somewhere, Salignat, our Frenchman, lived on remittances from his father, a grape-grower in Southern France. We also had dug up a Jap who had imbibed Socialistic doctrines, and duly set off for the hall where the meeting was to be held.

We had our platform arranged half an hour before the meeting was to start. 'Couldn't you give the platform a little more colour?' our secretary asked me. 'How so?' I replied. 'Why,' he said, 'you've got no coon.' Off I set, jumped, on the first tram car, got down to the purlieus of the docks, and soon ran up against a son of Africa. 'Say, have a drink?' I called to him. Sure he would.

* The speaker was Professor Walter Thomas Mill, who had been dismissed from the University of Wisconsin for his socialist views.

'Would he like to come to a meeting?' 'Anything for a shilling.'
He was on the rocks. So I got him on the street car and up to the
hall, and put him amongst the collection. And we had a most
interesting lecture, as our professor, in course of his remarks,
would turn to his platform friends, and say what country they
were from, and showed how their aims and aspirations could
only be satisfied by the ushering in of Socialism. Yes, it was a
great meeting, but after it was all over, and when I passed the
negro a couple of shillings, he wanted to know if he couldn't
sign on for a constant job. 'Anyhow,' he said, 'what was it all
about?' One gets great fun out of being a propagandist, and in
the earlier days a few knocks were thrown in.

At my very first attempt to speak in the open air, and at a
street corner in New York, when I was being subjected to a
sustained barrage of interjections from a loud-voiced member
of the audience, I was afraid of losing my temper and losing my
case by using the kind of language he did. At length he rapped
out, 'Why the hell don't you git back to "Hengland" with your
damned theories, if you don't like New York? What the gol
darned hell do you think we are to stand here and listen to a
foreigner telling us about our rotten government? Why don't
you git back to where you belong?'

Then an inspiration seized me.

'My friend,' I said, 'I am the only person in this crowd who
can prove, right here and now, that he has a right to live in this
country.'

'How so?' he demanded.

The crowd silently surged forward as I reached in my pocket
for my birth certificate, a copy of which I always carried with me.
'Here,' I said, 'is a document given to me by the legal authorities
of Boston, Mass., to show that I was born in that city in 1871.'

'Let me see it,' demanded my tormentor.

'No,' I said. 'Not you, but you, sir,' throwing it to a man on
my right, 'and you, sir,' to a man on my left.

And they assured the crowd that I was indeed a born subject
of their great and glorious mud heap. I had taken a chance that

no one else in the crowd was carrying a birth certificate.

'Now,' I called to the centre of the interruption, 'perhaps you will show us your birth certificate to prove that you yourself have a "right" to be, and speak, in the USA?'

'I don't have to carry my birth certificate,' he replied.

'Neither would I have to, if it were not for such ignorant folks as you,' I countered.

By this time the crowd, which as I find crowds do, liked to see an interrupter hoist by his own petard, began jeering at the 'patriotic' Yank till he retired, and we had a successful meeting. A successful meeting at that time was one where we got more converts than kicks.

In the South End of Liverpool, I was once holding forth to a small handful of listeners. It was hard going, for the opposition, a handful of lusty adherents of the now dead Member for that constituency, were trying hard to make me lose my temper in order to give them a chance to bash me. I was trying to show how, in my estimation, a man owed it to himself and family, as to the nation, to try to leave the world better for his having existed in it. Only the discontented made progress possible.

'Show me a contented man of the working-class,' I told them, 'and I will show you a hog, and point to the same man as you do.' 'Eh! now, now, Mister,' cried a massive-built man standing right under my nose as I was perched on the soap box. 'I am contented and I'm a working man.'

'I still adhere to my statement,' I replied.

'Call me an 'og, why don't you?' he kept calling out.

A friendly policeman on the fringe of my small crowd gave me the wink to wind up to save trouble, the time being just after eleven and some of my drunken fellow-workers now converging on us to have a laugh at those 'mad Socialists'. (This was about thirty years ago, and only this week, as I write this, a local slum-born boilermaker takes his seat as a Socialist to represent in Parliament that one-time Tory constituency of West Toxteth.) However, my meeting closed. I wended my way to my near-by home. But I was still pestered by my mammoth adversary. 'Go on, call me an 'og, call me an 'og' he kept repeating, keeping step with me and thrusting his evil face down into mine. I kept mute and walked on. Now I was conscious of other steps dogging ours. He had evidently an accomplice and they were waiting till I got to a dark neighbourhood where I was to be put through it, I thought. It was an ideal time and spot, for, except for our two selves and the phantom stepper some paces behind us, the streets were deserted. But an adjacent by-street evidently led to my enemy's home for he turned and left me after telling me what he would have done to me had I called him 'an 'og'.

Then the 'phantom stepper' accelerated his walk and caught up to me, and I recognized a hefty dock worker who had recently joined our little band of ardent disciples.

'Oh, Fred, Fred,' he called, 'Why didn't you call him a hog and let him hit you? I have been following you both. Fred lad, I can't talk much, I'll never make a speaker, but by God I can fight. I just wanted to do something for Socialism. And you spoilt me through not calling that bloke a hog. Why, Fred, if he'd hit you once, I would have smashed his face for him.' It was a fact our new convert was a well-known boxer true to the amateur class.

When I was working in Manchester I duly reported my presence in the town to the Central Branch of the Independent Labour Party. They were just discussing how to get a speaker for the following Sunday night at Tib Street corner in Market Street, and I was told off for the job. The time came, and I was holding forth when a loud roar was heard further up the street. My crowd soon dispersed to hear the new orator, Moses Moritz, speaking on behalf of the Socialist Party of Great Britain. All other Socialist organizations (to him) were 'backing up the Master Class'. The S.P.G.B. were the real cream in the coconut. Unknown to me Alec Thompson, 'Dangle' of the *Clarion*, was in my audience and commented in the following edition of that paper on the need for more unity and less heretic-hunting in our movement if it was to succeed, a fact as true today as ever.

A quaintly garbed individual in my audience took my attention and was pointed out to me as Stewart Gray: a year or two after this I ran across him again. It was in the Clarion Café in Liverpool. 'See what you can make out of that funny fellow in the corner there,' commanded our honorary club secretary, old Robert Manson. I recognized him and he unrolled a florid banner. 'Each man beneath his own fig tree' were the words embroidered in coloured silk ribbon on his flag. I took him home with me but in a couple of days I had tired of his mystic utterances. He was going to lead hunger marchers to London to demand reforms from Parliament, or die. He had a soul-mate in Southport who had a woman friend, who, he was sure, was my soul-mate. We were to march to 'the Smoke', heading the hungry procession, and he was sure that I would be an ideal second-in-command to him. I unloaded him eventually on poor Lipschinski, the artist. Three days or so afterwards I called on Lippy. 'Fred, Fred,' he said as soon as I entered his studio home in the garret of a deserted old church schoolroom, 'Why, oh why do you bring such funny men to see me?' 'I thought you wanted subjects for painting,' I said. 'Ah! so so, subjects not objects,' he replied.

But afterwards he was really pleased when I ushered the redoubtable Tom Mann, and later the fiery Jim Larkin, into his den and he produced wonderful portraits in oils of both of them. Eventually Stewart Gray did lead a contingent of 'out of works' to London. Refused admission at St. Stephen's, he lay down asserting he would die there ere he would shift, unless he was heard. However, the police carried him off and his crowd dwindled away, but no doubt their little pilgrimage through the country 'set people thinking', which, after all, is what agitators desire. From intelligent thinking comes intelligent action, and the higher realms of freedom, industrial, political, religious and social, can only be reached when more and more individuals realize that, in Mankind's plod from clod to god, it is compulsory to alter customs when customs connote compulsion.

I recall the occasion, about twenty years ago, when we got our first Labour victory in Liverpool. The voting was for Honorary

City Auditors.* For years and years these two representatives of the people were supplied by the Liberal and Tory parties without a contest. They each supplied one official and no reports of the City's income and expenditure were ever circulated. Our folks found this out, and proposed one of our very earliest propagandists (now John Wolfe Tone Morrissey, Alderman of the City of Liverpool). There were three candidates for only two positions, the voting paraphernalia had to be brought out. The Liberal and Tory local papers accused us of wasting public money by butting in, but we went on with our campaign.

I was sent with my one-time enemy, Jim Larkin, to do fly-posting around our mutual home area. Fly-posting, by the way, is sticking up surreptitiously small bills wherever one can do so without being caught, on such places as end walls, empty shop windows and hoardings. Our political opponents by their wealth were able to rent poster space, and fly-posting was our only means of meeting their activities. But the police were told off to detect us if they could. On this occasion Jim and I found ourselves outside a builder's yard where I was employed. It was right opposite an iron bridge which led into the road over the railway lines from the docks, and my boss's huge sign was an ideal place for our job. It was now after midnight. The yard was surrounded by a ten-foot wall covered with broken glass to keep out pilferers. Getting up on to the wall with half a dozen bills and a pail of paste and brush I was soon busy covering 'Charles Burt, Building Contractor' with exhortation to 'Vote for Morrissey'. I had a few cuts in my pants and on my hands when I had finished and handed the pail down to Jim, when his eagle eyes in the darkness espied a policeman coming towards us. He adjured me to lie low till he came for me, and cleared off.

I lay on that glass-covered wall looking into the starry sky for what seemed hours. The policeman's footsteps had long ceased

---

* This was rather more than twenty years before Bower's book was published in 1936. Morrisey was elected as auditor in 1901 – see P.J. Waller, *Democracy & Sectarianism: A Political and Social History of Liverpool, 1868-1939*, Liverpool University Press, 1981, p. 217.

to be audible. Frightened to move lest my figure might show on the skyline to the policeman who might even now be waiting against the wall beneath me, I thought of Wellington's 'Oh for night, or Blücher'. At long length I heard Jim's voice. 'I'm here, Fred. Be careful how you come down.' How sore I was, how sticky with paste on clothes and hair and features, how bloody with torn hands, but – how happy twenty-four hours after when we got the news that our man was in and Labour had at last broken the ice which eventually led to Socialist town councillors and M.P.s being elected in Tory Liverpool.

I had been speaking one night at a favourite stand called the Edge Hill Lamp. After the meeting a short middle-aged, grey haired man of middle-class appearance accosted me. He spoke of how he had enjoyed the way I had delivered the goods. 'They'll come to our way of thinking yet,' he said, by which I knew he was one of the elect. A few more words and we parted. Some ten minutes after this one of the comrades confided to me that the little grey man was the author of *The Ragged Trousered Philanthropists.** I had hoped to meet him again, but not long afterwards read of his death after a sojourn in one of our local workhouse institutions. But to have written a book such as his shows him to have lived a successful life, however and wherever he lived and died.

---

*   This was Robert Noonan, pen-name Robert Tressell, who died in Liverpool on 3 February 1911. The chronology is again suspect, with Bower jumping from the 1901 Auditor's election to 1911.

CHAPTER XV

'BLOODY SUNDAY'

AUGUST 13th, 1911, was an eventful day in the history of Liverpool.

The railway men's 'rank and file' strike, despite some of their leaders advising them to delay action and leave it to them to 'plead' with their masters, had been a success throughout the country. For over a week the railway system had been tied up, after sorry attempts to run a skeleton service by so-called students. By the way I cannot yet cease wondering how it comes, when a reform movement gets a move on in Britain, the 'students' always take the side of the conservative or backward forces, whereas in practically all other European countries the students are almost always on the side of advocates of reform. However, as I have said, the strike was on. Not an act of violence, not a stone thrown, not a worker was intimidated. It was a complete answer to the people who say the shareholders 'run' the railways, etc. Had every shareholder dropped dead in normal times, there would not have been a train late coming into Lime Street Station or leaving Euston. It was simply 'the one minute's silence' extended to the railway stations and yards.

On this Sunday in August, 1911, then, as the gaily decked banners, carried aloft by brawny arms, led each contingent of workers from the outskirts of the city, with their union buttons up and headed by their local officials with music, it seemed good to be alive. Of course some people were inconvenienced by the strike. It seems that only such inconveniences can make some folks take notice of the hardships which the toilers in mines, mills, factories and ships have to undergo in order to exist in this 'free' country. From Orange Garston, Everton and Toxteth Park, from Roman Catholic Bootle, and the Scotland Road area, they came. Forgotten were their religious feuds, disregarded the dictum of some of their clericals on both sides who affirmed the strike was an atheist stunt. The Garston band had walked five miles and their drum-major proudly whirled his sceptre twined with orange and green ribbons as he led his contingent band, half out of the local Roman Catholic band, half out of the local Orange band. Now, no longer were they the playthings of 'big business'. This day they were MEN. What matter to them that all the railway stations in the town showed boarded up gates? What matter to them, that from the windows and roof of St. George's Hall opposite, could now and again be seen the caps of a British Tommy? Never in the history of this or any other country had the majority and might of the humble toiler been so displayed. A wonderful spirit of humour and friendliness permeated the atmosphere. One almost felt that at long last the dispossessed and despised producers of all wealth were coming into their own.

It was glorious weather when, from a dozen wagons on the Plateau in Lime Street, speeches were being made in support of the railway workers who were asking for an increase of a shilling or two per week in their wages. The demand was only on behalf of the lowest paid, some of whom were expected to keep their families on as little as sixteen shillings per week. The higher grade men, such as drivers and firemen and foremen, had downed tools in sympathy. All was going well, no signs of trouble, when a well-organized mass, some forty thousand strong, ranged round the Plateau and surrounding approaches, all in their Sunday best, and many of them with their womenfolk with them, were set upon and brutally batoned.

From my wagon, facing the great St. George's Hall, I heard a rumpus behind me. It seemed a small skirmish. It afterwards transpired that two youths, sitting on a window-sill of the hotel opposite the Plateau on to which they had hoisted themselves, to see the better over the heads of the crowd, were brutally pulled off their perch by a policeman. A bystander quietly expostulated to the policeman on his roughness, and was himself roughly pushed. The constable had evidently got the wind up when others of the crowd booed him, and, drawing his baton, proceeded to arrest the man. An hour later, after the mounted police had cleared the streets, and all the hospitals in the city were filled with people with cracked skulls, 'peace' was restored for a time, only for trouble to break out again, as darkness came on, in the more depressed, and depressing, areas of the city.

At one end of the Plateau during the meeting the Pathé picture people had set up a machine and the operator was busy taking a moving picture of the monster demonstration. When the police started the bother and the crowd were hurrying to escape the batons, the operator kept on working. When the crowd dispersed he got away with his negatives. Had they been publicly exposed there would have been an out-cry of indignation throughout the land at the brutality displayed. The Plateau resembled a battlefield, disabled and wounded men, women and children, lying singly and in heaps over a vast area. The picture was privately shown to a few of the prominent Labour Leaders and speakers, but the Liverpool authorities and the Government warned the Pathé people that they were not to show the picture in public – 'or else'. At the subsequent 'inquiry' held to exonerate the police, which was a palpable farce, all evidence given by the demonstrators was pooh-poohed. One Labour man (now a Knight), telling at the inquiry how he saw a woman carrying a baby in arms clubbed to the ground, was asked, 'Why didn't you take the policeman's number?' It was like asking a soldier assaulting an enemy's trenches why he didn't lace his boots up during the charge, or something equally silly. The truth was, the police had perhaps (in fact, surely) unintentionally started it and had to see it through. A policeman can lose his head as well as a starved member of the community.

A protest meeting was called for the next Sunday. The speaker was Tom Mann. He was interviewed by the Head Constable and told the meeting must be called off. 'The meeting will be held even if you gaol a thousand of us,' said Mann.

'Then, if there is any trouble, I will hold you and the rest of the trade union leaders responsible,' replied the Chief . 'You keep your policemen out of sight, and there will be no trouble,' asserted the workers' leader. And there wasn't. And at the following November elections the Socialists gained a dozen seats in the council, and look like being, in a few short years from now, the predominant party. I was nominated and stood for the district I was brought up in, and had to contest the seat against an ex-Lord Mayor. It was a surprise the small difference between our votes, only 135 between us. This, in a True Blue stronghold of Toryism, where their citadel had never been attacked before. Since then, it has returned three city councillors, and an M.P. I contested the seat three times, then, realizing there might be an accident, and I might get returned, I refused to stand again. The squabblings and jockeyings in the political arena are not to my liking. I become more and more convinced that education is the only hope for humanity. I prefer to play the role of a minor teacher.

CHAPTER XVI

TRADE UNION DELEGATE

IN 1908, my union elected me one of the two delegates sent to the Trades Congress at Nottingham, and then one of the two delegates to the Labour Party Conference at Portsmouth. There I met most of the heads of the Labour Movement. Earnest and impatient, I sensed a laziness in many of my confreres who 'had arrived'. The ease of Parliament seemed to have emasculated most of them. I was amazed at the time wasted in 'fraternal delegates' speeches. Action, action, and again action, was what we younger men wanted. At Nottingham, we had to listen for an hour or two to delegates bringing 'fraternal greetings' from the Labour Party. At Portsmouth we had to listen for several hours to speeches of 'fraternal' delegates from the Trades Congress at Nottingham. Lucky was the newcome enthusiast, at either, who caught the Speaker's eye. Of course Bernard Shaw would. Hadn't the platform paid 2s. 6d. sometimes to hear him speak, and here he was, on his pins, asking to be allowed to speak. Of course he caught the Speaker's eye.

I am not writing out of pique, for, at Nottingham, I had been called on to speak. I don't now know what the resolution under discussion was, but I do remember telling the platform that we were wasting time, with our tuppence halfpenny unions fighting each other, instead of fighting the employers. I suggested the time would come when, instead of a parliament sitting, squabbling, and barging, over trivialities, we should have an industrial parliament of men, sent there because of their grasp of conditions in their own industry, to carry out the supplying of the necessaries of life, the production and transport wherever required, to represent severally Mining, Engineering, Transport, Agriculture, Building and Textiles. I remember the laughter and scorn I got from the platform, but I am as certain as ever that that way lies our route to happier times for the workers.

The year before this, Pete Curran had been returned for Jarrow. The day after the election I was told off to meet him at the railway station and bring him to the hall where we were giving a send off to old Keir Hardie, who was to sail next day for Canada. By the way, Keir Hardie was ever my beau ideal of a crusader. Often I have sat at his feet, in the hospitable old Labouchere's home, till the small hours of the morning, listening spellbound, as he described how the work was going on in the different parts he had visited. How we relied on the international spread of Socialism as being enough to stop any war between nations, and how we were mistaken, and how the thought of the failure of his over-sanguine dream broke the old warrior's heart, history has told. Keir, as I said, was off to Canada, the guest of a broad-minded admirer named Allan, of the Allan Line of Steamers. Knowing I took a glass of beer, and so did Pete, the Liverpool comrades sent a teetotaller with me to keep us from dallying. When we met Pete, he said: 'Where can we have a drink? I'm dry with travelling'. There was no pub on the direct route and I knew there was only a small house in a back lane reached by a side street. But our warder manoeuvred it so that we were in the hall before we knew it, and Pete only got coffee. He gave me a sad look, almost of contempt, which I never forgot.

After the meeting I was asked would I take a week's holiday and go down to Colne Valley, to help Victor Grayson in his Parliamentary campaign. The comrades clubbed my fare together, I being out of work, and I went down. There, I met again my old towny, Victor Grayson, who was always lecturing me on how much more good I could do if I did not drink. We had some happy chats that week. And how those mill folk worked. The day after the poll, I waited about noon in Slaithwaite, at the foot of the inclined street in which stood the Town Hall, from which the result was to be declared. Mrs. Pankhurst and her three daughters who, with the women suffragists, had worked like Trojans for our candidate, were in a car around the corner. A red handkerchief was waved from an upstairs window. It was the signal. We had won. I delivered the news to the wonderful woman and her daughters, and the hills resounded with the 'Red Flag'. It was a great day.

Some time after, I sat in a hotel in Chester, when in came Grayson, with Robert Blatchford, and Alexander Thompson, the playwright. I was introduced to them by Grayson as a Liverpool agitator comrade of his earlier days. Grayson's drink was whisky, and the others had to persuade him not to have any more. I thought how much better it would have been for him had he come in and had a glass of homely beer, instead of waiting for me as he used to do, when we were on our way to meetings at street corners in Liverpool.

Down at Portsmouth, then, I looked forward to meeting him again. He was to speak on a resolution which had been got on the agenda, for a more militant policy. Alas, when the time came, he was not there to speak. Not till next day did we learn that some young Tory bloods, professing friendship and sympathy with his views, had cajoled him into taking a run into the country, promising to get him back in time for the resolution. Whether they got him drunk or not, I can't say, but they kept him away.

About this time, I had been entrusted with the job of renovating some large marble slabs, on which were engraved the Lord's Prayer and the Ten Commandments. The slabs were let into the walls of a Liverpool church. A chum of mine being at that time at a loose end, I enrolled him in my staff. He knew nothing of the work, but there were certain jobs he could do without endangering the fabric. We had to work all night to get the work through. Slipping out to a near-by hostelry ere closing time, for a final, we ran into our mutual friend Lipschinski, the well-known portrait painter, and his good lady. They returned with us to see our work in the church. Lippy was a wonderful singer and soon his wife, at the organ, was accompanying him in 'The Lorelei'. It sounded glorious as the fine tones swelled through the almost darkened church, when a loud knocking was heard on the side door. Outside stood a policeman and a large crowd of people wanting to know what the row was about. I suppose organ playing in a church at midnight, except at the passing of the year, would seem to them uncomely. I asked the P.C. in, showed him our work, explained that the distinguished looking Lippy was a 'man sent up from London to tune the organ', and our man in blue retired taking his crowd with him. After our artist and his lady had gone home, my 'Staff' and I lay, 'each within his narrow bed', in the pews, for an hour or two's siesta. I little thought that my chum in the next pew, would in 1934 be Colonel Tom Tweed, author of *Gabriel over the White House, Blind Mouth,* etc. It's a long way from St. Emmanuel's church to a publisher's office, Tommy, but you arrived. Cheerio.

However, in June 1914, a strike, or rather lock-out, was on, in London, of the building trades. All men were refused employment unless they signed a note to say they would work alongside blacklegs. This 'document' ran

24 June 1914

To Messrs ......

I agree, if employed by you, to work peacefully with my fellow-employees (engaged either in your direct employment or in that of any Sub-Contractor) whether they are members of a Trade Society or not, and I agree that I will not quit your employment because any of my fellow-employees is or is not a member of any Trade Society; and I also agree that if I commit any breach of this agreement I shall be subject to a fine of Twenty Shillings, and I agree that the amount of such fine many be deducted from any wages which may be due to me.

Name

Address

No. of Unemployment Insurance Card

Witness

I took a holiday down there to speak on behalf of the labourers and try to raise a bit for them as their union funds were nearly depleted, for, if they were driven back, it might break up the morale of the others. I was sitting in the bar of the Cherry Tree and Mitre Hotel, in Chancery Lane, the headquarters of the London Strike Committee, when a stout, middle-aged man, with his wife, entered. I had seen him and thought to have some fun. But he also had seen me. 'Look at him, mother', he said to his partner, 'there's the man who got me parted from you for three months with his Open Letter', and he grabbed me round the neck in a friendly hug, and – we had something to drink. Tom Mann was off to South Africa next day, to speak at protest meetings against the deportment, to England, of half a dozen miners' leaders from Africa. At the railway station next day there was a huge crowd of well-wishers to see him off. Tom had to make a speech, and, in finishing, told the crowd there was a blackguard amongst them who had got him three months' imprisonment. 'And now', he said, 'I call upon that blackguard to get up here.' He got down, and I stepped up and gave a talk, when suddenly I noticed Victor Grayson there. 'And now', I said, 'I will call on another blackguard who got thrown out of Parliament through bad behaviour!' And Victor got up. But he was not the Victor I had known in the early days.

CHAPTER XVII

FIGHTING AGAINST THE WAR

HOWEVER, August 1914 arrived, and the 'blood bath' began. The document the London men had to sign, and wouldn't, was forgotten for more serious things. Right at the beginning of the war, I had made up my mind that the powers that be would not get me to kill a man. They could gaol or kill me, as they had the power, but I knew that it was not the workers' fight. Being born in a country does not make that country a man's possession, any more than being born in a certain house makes that house the property of the person born in it. By persuading the mass of the people in each country that it was 'their' country they were fighting for, the aristocracy had fooled the people through the ages. Wasn't it Dr. Johnson who said that 'Patriotism is the last refuge of a scoundrel?" Lloyd George himself has said, since the war, that he does not know what the war was caused by. The murder of the Austrian Archduke was only a pretext. Had it not been him, some other excuse would have been found. The war had to be, in order to stop German business from stealing the markets of the world, through superior technical and commercial efficiency.

That I felt and still feel. As a democrat, I claim to have a right to say what I will lay down my life for, if necessary. And I was certainly not going to do it to enable the landed and monied interests of this country to down the monied and landed interests of another. As a matter of fact, the spread of humanitarian ideals and socialistic principles, internationally, was going on at such a rate, that the 'owning' class were being tightly squeezed. Reading my history, with back copies of the *Times*, published when the Crimean War was on, I saw in the latter the fulsome praise lavished by the Press on the brave men in the Crimea. 'They will never be forgotten.' But hardly a week passed in my boyhood without reading of 'another Crimean Hero' dying in a workhouse. The same with the Boer War. The soldiers were all 'heroes' till the war was over, then, on the scrap heap with them, if they could not deliver the goods in the labour market. So, I knew, it would be in this last war, and we all know now the irony of the placards that covered our hoardings, showing a pretty house, set in a garden, and asking: 'Isn't this worth fighting for?' And we keep reading, day by day, of war veterans being turned out of slum-like dwellings, because they can't pay the rent.

We send men to Parliament, a cabinet is formed, to keep us out of war. They can't, or don't and, when the nations are pledged to the hilt to the bankers, and they see the supply of cannon fodder about finished, the same gang who couldn't keep us out of war, in each country, sit around a table, and settle to stop it. Now the way to stop a fire is to stop putting fresh fuel on it. In every country there were men who believed this, and who suffered for their convictions.

Mrs. Francis Adams, an American publicist, whose word was never challenged, was in Berlin when the war broke out. She reported that in Germany alone there were some three thousand men put against the wall and shot for refusing to take up arms against their fellow men. All countries, as I said before, had their share of these heroes. So some of us tried to save our fellow men's lives by getting the rulers (I don't mean kings and emperors, the money powers have these in their pockets) to listen to reason, and see if they couldn't be got to argue it out. It is fifteen years ago since the Armistice was declared, and for fifteen years the 'talking men' have been at it, 'settling the war'. How soon it will be before we are in another one, none can say, but, from all appearances, it won't be long. The only country that has found its soul in the whole business seems to be Russia.

However, in the early days of the war our meetings were dispersed, and the speakers rough-handled. It was: Believe what

Bottomley, and Lloyd George, and the *Daily Mail* say, or be
damned! It is not too hard to be a parrot, and repeat what your
masters and pastors tell you, and so, when they and the gutter
press said that Ramsay MacDonald, and Snowden, and those
who supported them in their views, were enemies of England,
there were always plenty of half-insane 'patriotic' hooligans to
show their bravery by smashing up honest (even if deluded)
speakers' meetings, in between rifling German butchers' shops.

I have such an overweening belief in the desire for good
action, which is more or less in all men's hearts, that I still believe,
as I did all through the war, that shiboleths and catchwords,
and superstition and ignorance, once relegated to their right
place, a truer understanding, a real feeling of the Fatherhood
of God, or Good, and the Brotherhood of Man, will manifest
itself amongst the citizens of the world. Therefore, my aim was
to help as many people who held the faith, to survive the war,
as I could. In Liverpool, I found the shipping companies were
stuck for men to man their ships, in the firing and stewarding
departments. Many Quakers and honest conscientious objectors
were supplied with bogus birth certificates, and discharges, and
shipped on as firemen. Some stuck to the job whilst the war
lasted, some cleared off in American ports. I can only think the
authorities winked at the proceedings, for their sleuths must
have known it was going on. And, in any case, the shipping
companies got their firemen.

It will be remembered that Australia, by a vote of the
population, refused to have conscription. The first time it was
voted on, the soldiers from the antipodes were not given the
chance to vote. Again, the vote was taken, and on this occasion
the Aussie soldiers, in the trenches, were given the vote. By a
huge majority, the soldiers voted against conscription. They
had had enough themselves. In Ireland, the British Government
dared not enforce conscription, for fear of having her hands,
already full up with trouble, further loaded. Hence, an Irishman
could come to England, and sign on as a fireman, sailor, or
steward, where an Englishman, Scot, or Welshman could not,

if he was of military age.

If a man came through with vouchers from certain organizations, to prove he had held anti-militarist views before the war broke out, and the committee in Liverpool, after sounding him, were satisfied of his bona fides, we made him into an Irishman, gave him a birth certificate to show his name was, say, P. Kelly, that he was born in some little hamlet in the wilds of Ireland, and this, together with a discharge note, to denote that Patrick Kelly had worked on the S.S. *Ruby*, 200 tons, Capt. John Burns, his mark X, and – he *was* Pat Kelly. A mate of mine, with his gear, was eventually locked up in London, and got six months' imprisonment, and that ended that. But we shipped some interesting cases.

During the war period Snowden often got up in Parliament to ask 'was it, or was it not, a fact that Russia had been promised Constantinople for a reward, if she came into the war'. And, each time, he was refused an answer, while the 'true blue bloody' Tory benches sneered and jeered at him. He had a reason for the question, for he knew the answer. And it does seem strange, that, in my dad's boyhood, 'we' were fighting with the Turks against Russia, to stop Russia from taking Constantinople. And here 'we' were, in 1914, fighting, with Russia on our side, to get Constantinople for Russia. In the Crimean War, our papers said, the Russians were fiends. In this war, they were heroes, until they took a tumble as to who were their real enemies, and then they were fiends again. In Napoleon's day, the French were fiends, the Germans, being on our side, angels. In 1914, the role was reversed. It seemed a case of 'when Father turns, we all turn', Father always being the ruling despot, whether as king or as a money power monopoly.

In the British embassy at Berlin, just previous to the war, we had a conscientious man acting in a minor capacity. He was aware of the understanding regarding Constantinople. He was too clean a man for secret diplomacy. Whether it was he, or another, told Snowden, and that knowledge led to Snowden's questions, I do not know. Anyhow, this man, high in office, bearing a military title, was put away for safety in a London gaol, early in the war. Here he met several more, who, without civil trials, were held prisoners for the duration. Amongst these, was a crippled man, who, for addressing 'Stop the War' meetings, was interned. These two, and another man, escaped from gaol. Two of them were recaptured and returned to gaol. The officer eventually died there. The cripple came disguised to Liverpool. I saw his photograph in a current copy of the *Mirror,* and a few hours after met him. I penetrated his disguise. There was a reward of £100 for his arrest. Going up to him, I put my arm on his shoulder and said: 'I arrest you for escaping gaol'. He blanched, but I put him out of his misery by winking. Taking him home, I rigged him in old sea gear. He was an artist, and proud of his long hair and clean hands. When I had cropped his hair off as close to the scalp as I could and rubbed charcoal into his finger nails, his mother wouldn't have known him. He almost cried as he surveyed himself in the glass. Getting another chap to sign on under the name of Farrell, we passed the signing-on note to the cripple. 'Now', I said, 'forget your Oxford accent, and do a bit of bloodying, or the regular men will tumble.' So I took him aboard the boat on which he was to be a fireman, the S.S. *Scythia.* He was a man who hadn't lifted anything heavier than a camera in his life, and I thought to myself: 'God help you, mate. You'll know what work is soon.'

Among his possessions was a parcel of which he was very careful. He offered to show it to me, but I was too busy at the time. It was, he assured me, the manuscript of an article written secretly in Pentonville by his officer friend, if I mistake not named Captain Malcolm Scott, whom I have mentioned as having been interned for knowing too much and saying too much. It seemed that in Scott's happier days he was deeply in love with a wealthy young lady from the Southern States of America. It was thought that could this story be got to the USA and published by her it would have a great influence in making the so-called 'statesmen' of the belligerent countries come to their senses and shorten the war. This document was thought too precious for the cripple to have upon him during the trip, for fear he was captured (which, as we will see, he was). It was therefore entrusted to a Quaker outcast whom I had smuggled aboard the same ship because of his faith in the holy words, 'They that take by the sword shall perish by the sword'. Whether the young lady of the Southern States got the package addressed her by Captain Malcolm Scott I know not. His tragic death perhaps has spoilt a wonderful war-exposure book.

However, half-way over to New York, an astute steward recognized my crippled comrade because of his deformity, and his photo in the papers. America was not yet in the war, and broke one of its own laws in letting the captain keep him in prison on the ship whilst the boat lay in a U.S. port, and he was returned to England, tried in Liverpool, made a speech in his defence which converted two listening warders to Socialism, and was duly returned to prison for the duration.

Meanwhile things were happening in Ireland. In Dublin the police seized the Transport Workers' paper, called the *Irish Worker*. One day, James Connolly came over to Liverpool to see me. Could I get him a hand press to run his paper on? I hustled round, but there was nothing doing. We went down into the town and I introduced him to some local Socialists. The question cropped up about Ireland's fight for freedom. Was the time ripe for revolution? This was the subject of discussion. 'Nothing near like', I said. 'How do you know?' asked Jim. 'Well, I think' – 'Never mind about what you think, what do you know?' I was searching for an answer when he continued: 'The only way to know when the time for any nation or any body of men to strike for liberty, is, to try it. If it succeeds, the time was ripe. If it does not succeed, the time was not ripe.' Of course I could only agree with his logic, and I thought back to Washington's affair in the American Colonies. Had Washington been captured by the British troops, and the revolution in North America quelled, Washington would have been hung as a 'rebel'. But, the revolution was a success, and, to this day, Washington is the 'Father of his country'. And a few years after the rebellion each county in Britain was trying to achieve some greatness to itself by claiming to be the birthplace of Washington, and his fellow 'rebels'-cum-'saviours'. So Jim Connolly returned to Ireland without his press.

A few days after this I was just retiring for the day, when I heard a knock on the door. Opening it I found a big rawboned man in working clothes who handed me a note. I read it and asked him in. Could I put him in the way of going to sea? He wanted to get to America. I soon sized him up. He was a giant in stature, as innocent as a child, and almost as simple. He told me his story that night after we had supped and dined, and it was two o'clock in the morning before I wended my way aloft after seeing him comfy on the sofa. Jim Larkin, in his introductory note, simply said: 'The bearer is a good man. Do what you can for him. He had had trouble.' And this is a true account of his story, a really pitiful one.

At the time of the Klondike rush, young and vigorous, he had gone out to America and took part in that mad scramble for gold. He hired himself out to other pioneers who had more cash than himself, and with them hiked over the Chilcot Pass. With over a hundredweight of gear fastened around him, he would set out; when tired, deposit it, and go back for some more. Then when all was got together, he would set off to a further point, and drop his load. Thus it was, going and coming, times and times again, till, after many days, he and his party made Dawson City. Jack London, whom he met there, and who was known to the boys as 'that writer chap', has told all about the Klondike in his books. Here our friend worked and saved. Saved every penny. And after a while sent over a hundred pounds to his old father in Ireland to buy a small shieling for himself.

Eventually he returned himself with two thousand pounds, and bought the farm on which he had worked as a boy. His father having died on the shieling, he gave that to his brother. His rough mining days had strengthened his views that there were only two kinds of women, the type that predominated in the rough mining camp, dancing with, or for the amusement of, the men, and – angels. But in his Irish home he met the village belle, some years younger than himself, and was carried off his feet. His brother, who had never left Ireland, tried to hinder him from marrying the girl, saying she was not good enough for him. But he married her, and, some time after, it came to his ears that his brother had been saying something to his wife's discredit. With the desperation of an honest but unworldly wise man, he went over to his brother's place, adjoining his own. He had always carried a revolver in the Yukon days. He had it with him now, and he shot his brother dead after an altercation. He never attempted to escape, was tried and sentenced to death.

Before he died, the priest (for he was a very God-and priest-fearing man) said, he ought to make his will, leaving all to his wife. This he did. But friends, feeling he had some cause for his action, got some members of the Nationalist Party to intercede in London for him. John Redmond was one of these M.P.s. Eventually, he was reprieved, and sentenced to life imprisonment. After seven-and-a-half years, he was released, but was not to reside within a certain number of miles of his farm for two years. His letters from his wife had got fewer and further between, and had almost ceased when he was released.

He broke his permit when he tried to see his wife and she refused to sell up and go elsewhere with him, or make the farm over to him when the time limit of his ban had expired. The police got to know he was at his place, and arrested him, and he was put in prison for some months for breaking his parole. And now, a broken man, he was trying to get back to America to forget it all. I was able to fix him up through a friend, and the last I heard from him was from a silver mine in Utah, USA, and told how he was fast pulling up and making good and forgetting certain things.

I had run over to Ireland to see how things were looking when I often met a daring little woman who was taking an active part in the industrial struggle, which, started before the war, was going on intermittently still. She was a vivacious, well-educated woman, the Countess Markievicz, born Miss Gore-Booth. She was energy every inch of her and of the sort who could inspire men to great deeds. Whether it was she who turned Jim Connolly towards Rebellion, I cannot say. But in his book called *Labour in Irish Industry*, he writes, 'Ireland can never hope to attain her freedom by armed force'. How came it, that, a few years after writing that, we find the brave-hearted (misguided, if you will) man, trying to do what in his book he said could not be done?

Not long after this, I had a visit from my old colleague, Jim Larkin. He was to sail to America and stayed his last night in Britain with me. Two detectives had shadowed him from Ireland, held watch outside my house all night, and were in evidence next morning following us to the boat. Jim had not long been in America when he was imprisoned on some flimsy pretext when America came into the war, and kept there till some time after the war was over. From Sing Sing gaol I got several letters from him, always breathing his faith in his Socialist creed. Some people, I believe, thought he should have stayed in Ireland and gone to his death with Connolly, but it had been adjudged best for him to go over to America and address meetings to raise funds for the Irish Workers' cause.

Sometime before he went to America, Jim had sent me an address in Liverpool where I was to call for six guns and ship them to Ireland. Being by now in a small tombstone business, I took a crate to the place and packed the guns carefully in the case, which I addressed on my business cards showing a tombstone printed on them, and labelled the crate 'Tombstone, With Care'. In the bottom of the crate was laid a slab of stone one inch thick, then the guns, then another slab an inch thick. This crate was handled at the Dublin docks by the men of Jim's union and I can see, knowing the sacred veneration the Irish hold for anything connected with the dead, how they would reverently handle the case so marked.

I always felt the idea of an armed rising was more of a threat, and the guns only to help the members of the Citizens' Army to acquire a military-drill training. However, as we know, it turned out something else. In any case, I felt that Larkin at any rate, knew that an uprising, with no other aim than to make a Republican Ireland, was no use to the workers, but would leave them still at the mercy of the capitalist class, as we know they still are in the Irish Free State.

In 1916, as the world knows, the short-lived Irish Rebellion took place, and the brave, kindly Jim Connolly met his doom. I think the men who composed the Government of Britain at that period would like to forget some of their actions at that period. However, there were many Irishmen who had fought against alien law, with a price on their heads. One man, with £500 reward for his capture, had got over to Liverpool dressed as a priest. The next day, disguised as a ship's fireman and smoking a short clay pipe, he was shipped and got away to America. I had made up my mind to help no army of workingmen to annihilate another army of workingmen, and, about this time, I had a paper calling me to be examined for cannon fodder. Seven years before, I had tried to get a job at my trade, on some buildings at the Sunlight Works. They wanted men, but I was too old. I was turned forty. I went down to the docks where I had worked once or twice before as a granite mason. 'Yes, I could have a job. What was my age?' 'Turned forty.' 'Sorry, can't start men over forty', I was told. And now, seven years after, I wasn't too old to take a gun to kill men whom I'd never seen, and, therefore, could have no grievance against. Just because some unknown, almost, scion of a so-called 'noble' Austrian House had been shot. A million British subjects lost their lives through the death of that wretched Dukeling. And it has transpired that there were only about seven men in Britain who knew that this nation had been made a party to an agreement to go to war with Germany if she invaded Belgium. The King of England was not one of them. And, it was only a few years before that our daily patriotic stunt papers were clamouring for us to go to war with Belgium ourselves over the red rubber atrocities. And only a few years earlier, when a certain big noise had said we, 'England', would roll France 'in blood and mud' over the Fashoda incident, if she didn't climb down.

And now, too old to get a job, I was to go against all my teaching and writing for years against wars, and join up. I had refused to take advantage of my age, and get a job on ammunition work. If I believed in war I would take a gun, not shelter myself and get big money making the guns. Friends had offered to get me jobs at good wages, overseeing the building of shell-handling works. I knew a few who knew no more about the work they were shoved into than my hat, but we all know how wires were pulled, and organizations used, by thousands, to keep men out of the trenches. So I simply went on cutting names on gravestones, from the beginning to the end of the war.

But – I had had a paper to 'come and be examined'. I put it in the fire, sold all my stock and sticks for a few pounds, and went for a walk, till the money powers said, 'This war must stop. All you nations owe us so much money, that, if it goes on much longer, we will never be paid, for there will be no more workers left to produce the goods, and buy back and consume the goods, by which means we get our own back, in profit, rent, and interest'.

It wanted a couple of months to Christmas 1918, when I found myself back in Liverpool.

The toy shops were already beginning to make a display of Christmas toys, and I did a tour round, to learn that old Daddy Xmas, the beloved of the youngsters, was not to be found. These toys had almost all been made in Germany, but the war had stopped this. So, hiring an empty shop, and purchasing on credit a two hundredweight bag of plaster of paris, I set up in business as a toy-manufacturer. To do this I had to get a permit from the authorities, which I did, but, toys not being necessary for war (except certain ones in time of peace, to foster the war spirit in children), I had to get a government permit to start a new business as a modeller. See me now busy turning out Daddy Xmases by the dozen. The shop had a plentiful supply of shelving, and in a week I had about a gross of 5d. ones, and three dozen 2s. 6d. ones, all dry and painted with gorgeous red coats and hoods, and black top boots. But I was up against a snag. I could not get stuff for the whiskers. Several toy shops had said they would take a few if I could deliver them a fortnight before Christmas. I tried to buy white rabbit skins, but rare as these usually are, they were not to be bought under a ransom at that time. They were in great demand, for the women's fur coats, which we heard so much about during the war, as being worn by soldiers' wives, sisters and mothers.

Meanwhile the time was going on. It wanted ten days for Christmas, nine days, eight days, and there the rows and rows of beardless Daddys were staring me, almost reproachfully, in the face. When an idea struck me, I never had much to do with babies, but I remembered seeing some furlike bordering on baby's bonnets. After trials, I found a shop which still had a few 'yards in stock, which I purchased with my last few pennies. This I cut into narrow strips, got my glue pot ready, and soon transformed my small army of legendary philanthropists. The change was marvellous. Not being a practical sculptor or modeller, my clay model, was, I am afraid, rather crude, and in my handling had got a decided squint. Anyhow we have no proof that old St. Nicholas did not have a squint, no more than we have that he wore Wellington boots. But it wanted now two days to Christmas. The shopkeepers who had promised to buy my output claimed they had no time in which to sell, and refused delivery. So I borrowed a handcart and hawked them around the streets, and, by Christmas, had sold enough to pay for the bag of plaster, and buy myself a Christmas blow out. The rent? Oh, I forgot that, or rather left enough squinting Daddys on the shelf to pay it, when and if the landlord had hawked them around and sold them.

Thus ended my first and last attempt to be a millionaire toy-manufacturer.

The war was ended for a breathing space, but the settlement of it still goes on, only to break out again shortly, if certain interests and individuals in the combatant countries have their way. Of course there may – most likely will – be a re-arrangement of forces. We may yet see a British Army being used to put back a Hohenzollern on the throne of Germany. Or a desperate attempt being made to hinder Russia from the attainment of her ideal.

CHAPTER XVIII

GOLD DIGGING IN AUSTRALIA

BUT, the war ended, I thought I would take a run over to Australia. Through a certain channel, I was able to sign on, at 48 years of age, as a 'boy' on the Blue Funnel liner S.S. *Nestor*. We left Glasgow and picked up some 1500 troops at Falmouth. They were home-returning Aussies and New Zealanders. My job was to assist in cleaning and clearing up the decks in the morning. In the hot weather it was so stifling down below that as many men as could do so slept on the deck. I had to run along and call to them to wake up. If they were too slow the sailors came along with their hoses and they were in for a wetting. After breakfast my job was mixing paint, down in the fore peak, under the charge of 'lamps'.

I enjoyed the life, the men were a jovial, intelligent lot, and put up with my preachments without trying to combat my arguments. We put into Cape Town, and into Durban, but all public houses were closed to the Australian soldiers. Previous ships' passengers, returning soldiers, had played such devilish pranks that while a troopship was in port all saloons were closed by order. On Armistice Day anniversary, each man was allowed to buy one bottle of beer on board, and no more.

The time was spent by the studious passengers in listening to lectures given by padrés, army surgeons and officers, but most of the men spent their time playing 'Crown and Anchor' or 'Housey Housey'. I let it be known to the officer promoting the lectures that I had the gift of the gab, and would take a turn at the talking game if they would care. It was just what he wanted. The men were long sick of listening to the goody-goody stuff. And so it was arranged, and duly chalked on a large black-board on the main deck, that 'Deck-Boy Bower' would speak on 'Evolution'. I was a favourite with the soldiers. The war had made a great percentage of them Socialists, or inquirers into the meaning of things. I had got permission from the chief officer to have an hour or two off my work, and got going. For over two hours I rattled on, drawing a mind picture of the scientific conception of the formation of the earth, the coming of life, flora and fauna, to man, his stages through Savagery, Barbarism, Serfdom, to the present, and the tendency to the Cooperative Commonwealth of the future. My sailor pals were proud to see one of themselves holding a meeting of officers and men in attention.

The outcome of the meeting was that a debate was arranged. 'Was Socialism possible or desirable?' My opponents were a colonel and a sergeant. On my side, I was supported by a young subaltern, who had been converted in the trenches. The chair was taken by the ship's doctor, Doctor Brown. At the finish, when a vote was taken, all hands went up for our side. It was one of my joy days. I told the men they were going back to flags and banners and banquets, but in six months' time many of them would be out of work and hunting a job. I knew it. I had seen the aftermath of the Boer War. They were heroes when they were killing Dutch farmers, so that the Rhodeses and Robinsons and Barnatos and Beits could own the diamond mines undisturbed. But, when they got home and got their finery off, and put on their corduroy trousers, and looked for a job, they formed a section of the unemployed army, they were no longer heroes, they were a 'menace', or, at any rate, a 'problem'. And so it was that bands met the ship, and – well, you will know the glad, and sometimes sad, home-comings there were in those days.

I had signed on to Adelaide, and there I said 'goodbye' to my shipmates, and sought out my brother's widow and kiddies. He had died two years before. I got a job and stayed with them. Each Sunday saw me holding forth at the Botanic Gardens, the Hyde Park of Adelaide. And even on the second Sunday, several of the men who had been passengers came up to me after the meeting and said already my words were coming true. They couldn't get jobs. I found Australia a glorious country to live in, if one could live without working. But work was as precarious there as it is here. In fact, there is no country in the world which has not an unemployment problem, unless it is one in which chattel slavery exists. In Adelaide, for anyone in the building trade, it was a week's work, and two weeks out of work.

I soon made friends, and around about Christmas 1920 I joined a few men who were going prospecting for gold. There is a lot of glamour about gold getting, but in the big mines, where most of the gold comes from, the gold diggers are much like navvies at home. They pick and blast the rock, and much of it shows in the rock, not a streak of gold. This is put through a process of crushing, till it is like soft mud. Gold particles, being the heaviest, sink to the bottom of this pulped rock, and are extracted by a cyanide process. But the 'place' miner is a smaller affair. One buys a 'miner's right' for five shillings. This permits a man to dig on any unoccupied government lands in the out-back, or bush.

So behold four of us setting off with picks and spades and tucker, and a miner's cradle or bowl, like a large sized wash-bowl, but with an indentation stamped in it a few inches from the top. After leaving the rail head, we tramped some miles into the woods, along a well-beaten road, to a deserted digging. Here we found numerous holes about four feet square, and anything from a couple of feet to six feet deep. These showed the place had been worked at one time, so we set to, opening out other holes. We were the only prospectors in that district.

Day after day we dug out the holes till we got down to the hard rocky reef. Here, we would take up the last foot of earth, or sand, or pebbles, and, in bags of about a hundredweight, carry it some half a mile away, to the only water we could locate, a muddy pool, about fifteen foot across and two feet deep. Here we fill our dish, and, covering the contents with water, rock or swirl it from side to side at an angle. The groove I mentioned was to give the water a swirling movement. Then the man using the pan or dish would stop, take off two or three handfuls from the top and throw it away. A few more swirls and some more top stuff would be thrown off. At last there would be left a small deposit of black dust like iron pyrites. If there were any specks of gold, they would show now. We had fixed up our tents the first day. One could cut as much timber as one wanted, and we cut some small stuff, knocked up stretchers to keep us off the ants and spiders, and rigged our beds of leaves with which we filled the sacks we had taken with us. One of our party had been on the game before and he knew where there was a trickling spring a couple of miles away. With our canvas buckets, we loaded up and got our billys, or cooking pots, going.

Our tent consisted of a large back scene from an Adelaide theatre which was deemed too worn and painted over to be again used and was thrown out. This, acquired through the friendship of the theatre props-man, depicted a view of the Alps dotted here and there with vivid red-roofed chalets and a cluster or two of deep-green pine or fir trees. Sitting or lying inside our tent during our siestas in the noon hours, with the heat outside at boiling point, it made me feel almost cool looking up to our roof with the sun shaft sending through it its lighting and searching rays and made our humble habitat look quite a grotto. But, on the third night, an unusual (for the time of year) and terrific downpour of rain attacked our gorgeous canopy. Very soon the rain had washed through the old and worn canvas. To go outside was to be soaked to the skin, so we lay under our blankets and chortled or cussed, as the spirit moved us.

Next morning we were a bonny sight. Scotty, our guide, our old-timer, had his face, neck and chest a beautiful vermilion, where the colouring had left the red tiled roof of a chalet to settle on him, lying underneath. Our engineer chum was a glorious green from the emerald-tinted foliage. I had been couched 'neath a glacier and was spangled like a herring with some silvery substance like mica, which had given the glacier an ice-like appearance. But for the rest of our stay, our sky (inside the tent) was unclouded and we could study the form of the

Southern Cross and its attendant star clusters, as through an old-time Nottingham-lace curtain.

I won't dwell too long on the gold-digging days. It's too painful. At the end of ten days, working eight to ten hours a day, digging and carrying and panning, the four of us got just three specks of gold. This, in a field where, rumour had it, men had made money at the game. The three specks were put into a small bottle of water. At the end of the tenth day, our guide, a Scottish bricklayer, pulled out the bottle, shook out the specks on to a white piece of paper, and we looked in turns at them through a powerful microscope. They looked as big as kidney beans and a glorious yellow, when one of the boys who was looking at them sneezed, and blew the specks into the grass. We looked at each other. Then laughed. Laughed heartily. Had there been any pub around, I, for one, would have got drunk. A load was off my mind. To me, it had been like everything else in my life, an adventure, but the others, I felt, really wanted to find gold. Each day I had suggested chucking it. It looked too much like work for my liking. 'No. We might strike a nugget in the next hole we open', they said. But that sneeze settled it.

The next day I took the gun into the woods to try and shoot a parrot. They were pretty green birds, flying in groups of about a dozen, with a screeching noise. I couldn't get a pot at one that day. They are counted good eating, I had heard, and wanted to try. But I had just looked up, to see two large grey birds, the size of large pigeons, flying towards me. I let fly and wounded one which crashed at my feet. I put another shot into it to put it out of its misery. Its mate flew daringly near me, as if about to attack me – when I saw what I had done, I had shot the protected bird of Australia, the Cookaburra, or Laughing jackass. There is a heavy penalty imposed on anyone shooting these birds, as they are supposed to keep snakes down. There are government wardens in certain districts, to see the birds are not molested, to watch for fires, and to see that the diggers' claims are not jumped, etc. Picking up the dead bird, I placed it in a hollow tree stump, and got back to camp. The next day I went over to look at it. Nothing remained but feathers and bones. The ants had cleaned these of every bit of flesh, and it might have been lying there for twenty years. A day or two to wait around, and yarn, and smoke, and rest our aching backs, and we returned to Adelaide.

Soon after, I saw my old boat, the *Nestor*, was lying at Port Adelaide, some nine miles away, which is the port for Adelaide. I ran over to see the boys. The outcome of this visit was they prevailed on me to take a run to Melbourne with them. Being out of work, I stowed away. Hiding from the officers, I got to Melbourne unseen, and had to get ashore. The Prince of Wales, on the *Renown*, was at Port Melbourne, and that ship was moored close to the *Nestor*.* Everybody going aboard, or leaving the dock from, the *Nestor* or *Renown*, was questioned. However, I got my sailor's bag, with a few mason's tools in it, ashore, by a bit of manoeuvring, and, next day, I got a job on the extension to Melbourne University.

Here in Melbourne the speaking was done on Sundays, on the banks of the Yarra River. Every Sunday, religious, political, and Socialist meetings were held. The 'Yarra bank' is the Hyde Park of Melbourne. Here, I met many men from parts I had visited, and made many friends. I was six months in Melbourne, then returned to Adelaide and on the first Sunday was back at the old pitch in the Botanic Gardens. After my speech, a tall, hefty man called me aside. 'Would you go to Russia?" he asked. 'Go anywhere,' I said. 'Well, I've heard you speaking. If you could go to Russia, and see how things are going on there, then come back and tell the people here, you could do good work', he went on. He unfolded his plan. I was to get to England how I could. He would give me an address in England I was to call at, and there somebody would take me to a boat and introduce me to the captain who would take me as a passenger. In Russia I was to report at Moscow, and would be shown all there was to see and given a ticket back to Australia, and accommodation would

---

* Edward, Prince of Wales, toured Australia between April and August 1920.

be supplied for me in Moscow. It sounded like an adventure, and I was on it.

I had saved about four pounds, so, buying a railway ticket, I got to Sydney. Here I had a job to get a ship. Each Sunday I spoke on the 'Domain', the outdoor forum of Sydney. But my money was done. I only had to tell the boys and they would have helped me, but I always have had an abhorrence of using my comrades in my adversity. I remember my last meeting, under a huge fig tree, in the 'Domain'. The local comrades gathered a collection of several pounds towards supplying free literature, and, that night, I slept under the fig tree, not having the price of a bed. But sleeping out is no hardship in Australia. Professor Goode was speaking in Sydney Town Hall. He had been in Russia during the revolution. He spoke as an educationalist. After the meeting I had a talk with him, when Tom Walsh came up. He is, or was, the secretary of the Seamen's Union. His wife I was introduced to, and I reminded her of the day when I took her and her mother and sisters the news of Grayson's victory at Slaithwaite. She was Mrs. Pankhurst's youngest daughter, Adela. It was good recalling old days.

Being in Sydney, I thought I would get to know all I could about Russia. Making inquiries, I found there was a Russian consul, and dug him up. He was an unassuming young fellow who had rented an office off one of the main streets near the railway station. He had had no money from any source and was as poor as any church mouse, but full of spirits and enthusiasm. His was one of those unpronounceable names which most Russians have, ending either in *ski* or *itch*, but I knew his first name was Peter, and Peter and I got to be good pals.

In conversation the name of Brookfield came up. Brookfield was the sitting Labour M.P. for Broken Hills. When in town he shared digs with Peter. As he hailed from the same part of Liverpool as me, I was anxious to meet him. 'He will be coming down tonight,' said Peter, 'and I will introduce him to you.' I was delighted and we went on to talk of other things, when we heard the newsboys outside shouting: 'Well known M.P. shot!'

Running out to get the paper, we found it was our guest-to-be, Brookfield. He was on his way to Sydney when his train pulled into Bendigo. Here a passenger sprang out of his seat on to the platform, brandishing a revolver. Everybody ducked and hid for safety. Seeing the poor fellow seemed demented Brookfield went to grab him and disarm him, and was shot dead. His murderer was arrested. In the coroner's court, later, it came out that he was a Russian miner from Broken Hills. There, in his room, the walls were found to be adorned with pictures of Lenin, Trotsky, and of poor Brookfield himself. A verdict of death through 'being shot by a madman' was brought in and the culprit was to be detained during his Majesty's pleasure, or whatever words the same thing means in Australia. Tears were in Peter's eyes as I left him.

CHAPTER XIX

SHIP'S FIREMAN, AGE 50*

EVENTUALLY I got a ship and signed on as a fireman on the Australian Commonwealth steamer, the *Bakhara*. She had belonged to the Germans, but had been taken from them during the war. The boys were pretty decent and I, being green, was given the job of Peggy. Now a 'Peggy', to the uninitiated, is the 'Mary Ann', or 'slavey', for the rest of the firemen. My job was to get the grub for the firemen and trimmers out of the stores each day, and the cooked food from the galley, wash up and scrub the tables, forms, and floors of the men's living quarters, etc. The day we sailed from Sydney, that town was being paraded by banner-bearing unemployed demanding 'Work or Bread'. Some thousands of workless followed the banners. And, at that very time, the shipping companies and certain interests in Britain were advertising what a glorious country for the workers was Australia.

We set off then, as I thought, for Britain. But our first stop was at Napier in Tasmania. Here some dozen men boarded us, trying to get home to Britain, willing to work their passage at any and everything. Tasmania, I found, had also its unemployed problem. From Napier, where we loaded up with apples and butter, we moved on to Burnie. Here we found flags were waving. We marked a red letter day in the history of the town, as we were the first big ship to enter the harbour and tie up at their new jetty. Here we took some more apples and butter aboard, and had a few more men seeking to get back to England and, as

---

* Bower was born in December 1871, so this must be around late 1921 to 1922.

they hoped, employment. From Tasmania we worked back to Australia and put into Port Melbourne.

Again the ship was besieged with unemployed seeking to work their way back to the homeland they had been fooled from. One of them was lucky. He had been out in the colonies six months. Carried away with the rosy picture drawn by the emigration people in Scotland, he had chucked up his job as a street car driver in Glasgow and come out, meaning to send for his family later on. In six months he had worked two weeks with a 'cocky', up country. A 'cocky' is a small farmer. Fed up with working from dawn to dark for one pound per week, and living like a barbarian, he had quit and gone back to Melbourne. Here he used his membership of the Freemasons to see the mayor of Melbourne, and in half an hour was on the ship and duly signed on as an assistant steward.

From Melbourne, then, to Adelaide again. Still they came, men trying to escape to England, and perhaps work, from a beautiful climate and no work. Then we moved on to Freemantle, and whilst there I took advantage of the visit to run over to Perth, some dozen or so miles inland. Here I met and had a chat with Miss Prichard,* the well-known Australian novelist whose husband, Captain Throstle, VC, had made a great sensation by denouncing all wars on returning to Australia, and publicly vowing he would never again be fooled into war. And, of course, being a VC the stay-at-home 'patriots' couldn't very well call him 'coward'.

Next morning we sailed from Freemantle, and sailed a man short. Our leading fireman, having dallied too long with a fair maid of Perth, had missed the boat. This necessitated firemen working what is called 'deucers' or six hours instead of four, in turns. For this the men got 2s. 6d. an hour overtime, but only a fool would want to be a fireman, and only a damn fool to work six-hour watches as a fireman. So the boys prevailed on me to go below and trim coal. I had never been down a fire-

* Katherine Pritchard was a novelist and founder member of the Australian Communist Party.

hole before. Enough for me had always been a view through the gratings from the deck. But, 'try everything once' said my imp of venture, and I approached the chief engineer and asked to be allowed to go down trimming. He looked at me as though I had lost my senses.

But I was duly installed down below, and right here and now I want to say if any minister thinks he's going to scare a ship's fireman by talking of the heat of hell into being 'good', he's got another think coming. Tell him it's a cold place and he might be scared into salvation, but heat – never. My brother having died as I have mentioned earlier, and having been a sailor at one time, I had taken his discharge book and name, and age. This made me about 37 years of age, whereas I was turned fifty, and rheumatic fever twice had left me with a weakened heart. Suffice it to say that the three weeks I spent in the fire-hole of that ship burned it into my brain. In fact I suffered so much that I hate now to recall it and won't dwell on it.

When, between the below watches, I tried to tell my mates of the advantages of oil fuel burning, they were for putting me 'into the ditch'. What the hell was I talking about? Only six firemen would be wanted on this ship, what was to become of the other twenty-seven? At one point of our journey we did have a spell for a few hours. We were running short of coal. Picks were provided to break up an accumulation of dust and small coal in the bunkers. This had been in when the ship had been taken from the Germans during the war. It had coalesced into concrete with dampness. And so we had to be Colliers digging for our fuel.

One of the boilers was giving trouble, also, so the captain ran out of our course a bit, to where the undersea chart showed land, not too far beneath the waves. Here we fathomed, and eventually put sea anchors out, and stayed to effect repairs. Some of us baited a giant hook and fished for sharks, but they wouldn't bite. Repairs over, in about eight hours, we set off again for the halfway house, the Cape. And here, in Durban, I went on strike. I told the chief I wasn't fit to do the work.

'Then why did you sign on?' he asked. 'To get home,' I replied. The shore steward and purser and chief held a court martial. 'They could gaol me for refusing duty'. 'All right. Get on with it! Gaol would be heaven compared to working in the bowels of the *Bakhara* again,' I told them. 'Are you a fireman?' asked the shore steward. 'No,' I said, 'I'm a sailor.' My discharge book, or rather my brother's which I was using, was produced. 'Yes, your book shows you are a sailor, then why did you sign on as a fireman?' 'Anything,' I said, 'to get on the sea, back to my home port.' 'But you are only young. You should be able to stick it,' 'I am fifty turned," I said, unthinking. 'Your book only puts you down as thirty-eight,' said the purser. 'I gave a wrong age when I first went to sea, in order to get a ship, and I've had to stick to it ever since.' The lie came glibly to my lips. Eventually poor Scotty, the car driver, who had been 'promoted' to Peggy whilst I was 'promoted' to fireman, was again 'promoted' to fireman, and I was put back to my original 'Mary Ann job'. However, Scotty only worked two or three days as fireman, when we put into Capetown, and he was relieved by the chief taking a man out of the dozens that again besieged us, trying to work their way back to England and hoped-for work.

At Capetown, at the Queen's Head Hotel, just outside the dock gates, I entered with some eight pounds I had drawn for wages. On the government-owned Commonwealth Line boats a sailor can draw his pay once a month if in port. Hence I drew mine. The strain I had gone through was so severe that I wanted to forget it. Entering the pub, I called for drinks around. As in every seaport all over the world, there are always plenty of down-and-outs, hardups, bums and scroungers, holding up the walls of a pub, either inside or out, and so 'twas here. 'Fill 'em up again, boss,' I called. Sequel: I was picked up blotto outside the pub an hour later by my shipmates, carried aboard, put in my bunk, and slept for twenty-four hours. I hadn't a copper left of my eight pounds, but the rest, mentally and physically, was worth it.

And when I did wake up we were off on 'the last trail'. We

were not a passenger boat, but had six or seven passengers aboard. One of these was a fine smart fellow who had been an officer in the Air Force during the war. He had received a bullet in the brain at a spot where it was dangerous to operate. Son of a wealthy cotton-mill owner in Lancashire, he had been shipped to the colonies hoping the change would do him good. But it was of no avail, and now, we understood, he was travelling home to undergo a last-hope operation, in one of the large London hospitals. At times he was quite rational for several days together, then he would break out and in his dementia he was not responsible for his actions and his language. We all felt sorry for him for he was a fine type of young man. His cabin was on the orlop deck, where he had his two paid attendants who were to see him to England and never leave him till then. Night and day, the attendants took turn and turn about. The fore-part of the ship had been netted up to some eight or ten feet. This, he was given to understand, was to stop the cricket ball (a chunk of rope ends tied as near round as possible) from going overboard, and everyday the officers not on duty played cricket with him.

One day, in between his spasms, he had told his attendants that he knew what they were there for, but he would go overboard in spite of them. A few days out from Capetown, he had eaten his dinner, seemingly quite normal, when he rose suddenly as if to go to the lavatory, and rushing out of the cabin, before his attendant could stop him, lifted up the netting, which he evidently must have cut unbeknown to anyone, and dived over the side.

We had been followed for several days by sharks looking for victuals thrown overboard after meals. The cry rang out 'Man overboard!' The ship was pulled up and turned in a narrow circle. Lifebuoys with flare lights, which contained some chemical substance which became ignited on touching water, were flung from the captain's bridge, lighting up the dusk which in these latitudes so soon gives way to darkness. One agonizing shriek we heard, to be cut off staccato as he was seized and drawn under the waves by the sharks. Then all was silence. Two boats were lowered and pulled towards the flares, whilst the ship was stopped and all eyes peered into the darkness. For an hour or more we lay there in the inky blackness. Not another light, or sign of life, appeared on the ocean except the two boats that had pulled around as near as possible to the locality where the poor fellow had dived over. At length the skipper called the boats in, and we got going again. But it was several days before the ship's company could shake off the gloom the affair had shrouded us in.

Eventually we reached the Mersey, and soon, with meeting friends and relatives, the affair would be counted just one incident of a rover's life. Whilst coming up the Mersey, I took advantage of an idle spell to fling my old clobber overboard. They were in rags, and stained with grease and oil. Trim and tidy, I was soon paid off on landing. But I had sewn the piece of paper with the address on it, which I was to call at to get a free pass to Russia, into the hip pocket of the pants I threw overboard. And now I had had my journey from Australia for nothing. However, I travelled to London and met many of the Labour people whom I thought could help me to locate the person who could, I had been told, pay the fare to Russia for anyone who wished to see industrial conditions in that country for themselves. But, like the famous Mrs. Harris, there was no such person, or, if there was, I could not run him to earth. So I never got to Russia after all.

CHAPTER XX

CARAVAN AND HUT

I WAS worn out, and, getting back to Liverpool, I found sanctuary in the studio of an artist friend, John Pride.* It is now pulled down to make room for an addition to Liverpool's largest department store. Here, for some months, I eked out an existence running messages, tidying up, and doing odd jobs. At the end of that time, an old journalistic friend, Jimmy Eastwood, blew in from the Channel Islands with his wife and young child. He had been on the staff of one of the Liverpool papers before the war, during which he had served in the 4th Cheshire Regiment, and also acted as courier between England and France. He had developed consumption, and had been advised to get into a more favourable climate. So he had taken a billet as private secretary to Compton Mackenzie, the novelist, in his island home of Herm. Through some difference of opinion they had parted and he had come north again. A friend soon got him fixed up with rooms, and I continued my life at the studio at the top of the four-story building.

The studio had a roof light, and on a beam running across the room was a short rope hanging. I was curious to know what it was for, and John Pride, the artist and poet who rented the studio, told me. Before he had taken it over, the studio had been shared by two painters in oils. They worked for themselves. One managed to make a poor living having a standing order for two or three pictures per week of Highland cattle drinking

* John Pride, artist and poet, born in Edge Hill, Liverpool, and direct descendant of Colonel Thomas Pride, who expelled royalists from Parliament in Pride's Purge, December 1648.

in a stream, from a local picture dealer. The other could not seem to sell a picture, and one day his friend came up into the studio and found him hanging – dead. He got a step ladder and cut him down, and the noose over the beam with a foot or so of rope hanging from it was the last thing I saw at night and the first thing in the morning, my couch being right underneath it. I used to get some fine themes for thought out of the sight of the suicide's loop.

Then came the time when my journalist friend, James Eastwood, was ordered away again for his health and I went with him to the seaside to act as medical attendant, friend and adviser, and general factotum, for my grub. Ultimately he recovered somewhat, and I was able to leave him and get to work on additions to Ruthin Castle in North Wales, which historic place had been sold by the Cornwallis West people, for a high-class hydro. I was now pretty well myself again and in a few months' time moved on to a government job, a post office, in Rochdale. But a lock-out on the job sent me to a waterworks job on Blackstone Edge for the Oldham Corporation. Blackstone Edge is a Saddleback hill, dividing Lancashire from Yorkshire. Here I made my residence at the White House Inn, the only habitation for several miles in either direction, and the 'pull up' for wagon and charabancs. Here I was in my element, meeting in the pub at nights the charabanc parties of factory operatives returning from Blackpool.

I had cut the letters R.T. in a rock built into an outhouse, and would confide to the visitors that Dick Turpin had stayed in the old inn, on his famous ride to York. How he got so far out of his way, I didn't know, or care. Anyhow, I was never asked. Picking up a lantern, I would show them the famous initials which I had smudged to look ancient. 'Eh, lass! It's reet what the old man says. Look theer. Sithee. R.T.' 'And that's Dick Turpentine's doing, eh, owd `un?' 'Turpin, not Turpentine,' I had to say more than once. 'Eh now, but shouldn't that R be a D for Dick if he cut it?' 'Well, no. You see, Dick is the short for Richard' 'Of course. Ah know. Ah'm nobbut pullin' tha leg, owd 'un.'

And then we would return to the hostelry, whilst I would weave romance into the neighbourhood which would make Sir Walter Scott envious were he in the company. And going out to climb on the charas again, there would generally be some old dame to whisper 'Eh, lad, but tha's a bonnie leear.'

But the wanderlust took me away to a country village by the Deeside, and here I thought I would find an anchorage and live on my memories. Seeing a caravan for sale in a local paper, I acquired it, and now, at last, lived in my own house. For a few pounds per year rent I got a small piece of ground in a field to place it on, and soon had an enclosed garden around it and could sit when my work was done, and soliloquize. The caravan was a discarded Liverpool Black Maria which had been used to carry prisoners to Walton Jail, after receiving their sentences at the City police court. It had carried more than one murderer to the place of his execution. I used to try to imagine the feelings of some of the poor wretches, as they took their last ride. And here I wrote:

It's an eerie place, a leery place,
Where I rest my bones o' nights,
And watch the moving moonbeams pace
The length of the louvred lights.
Yet it talks to me with abandon free,
Of unwilling guests it has held,
Of a lust-mad youth, Who, with terrible ruth
To a rape, cruel death did weld.

Twas an eerie place, and a dreary place,
To those who did take their last ride,
To the gaol on the hill, to be prisoned until,
The hangman stood tense by their side.
With the parson a-sighing, the prayers for the dying
(The bolt's drawn!) Then – prayers for the dead,
And a once-loved and beautiful mother's child,
Is at rest in a quicklime bed.

Twas a dismal place, an abyssmal place,
To the caught and convicted thief,
Whose plea of duress, and of hunger's stress,
Failed to get him the hoped-for relief,
But who can tell what a vision of Hell,
It appeared to the wayward maid,
Who, essaying to roam from a loving home
Is first "caught" while plying her trade.

It's an eerie place, a leery place,
Where I rest my bones o' nights,
And watch the moving moonbeams pace
The length of the louvred lights,
But I like to think that those who rode,
Were no better, nor worse, than me,
That their prison van, is but my abode,
Is inscrutable Fate's decree.

My journalist friend had in the meantime grown worse in health and as a last hope his friends got him to a famous sanatorium at Montpelier in Southern France. But the fell disease had got too fierce a grip on him, and his wife, now a rising novelist, was notified a few months later that if she wished to see him alive she had need to come quickly. However, despite her hurry, she arrived too late.

In my caravan home there was no happier man than me, but the neighbourhood was not too pleased with caravans and bungalows stuck about, and a move was made to shift them by the authorities. I held out to the last, but one day came the blue papers to tell me I was to be fined one pound per day if I was living in my caravan after two weeks' time. And thus, the very first time in my life that I wanted to settle down, I was not allowed to.

I was always a welcome guest to the grave-diggers in a cemetery when erecting or lettering a memorial, and at noon in their bothy or cookhouse there were few more jovial fellows. Their work may (and undoubtedly does) make them contemplative, but as a rule they have no illusions about the dignity of the burial service. At one town-owned cemetery where I often worked we had a whimsical digger called, shall we say – Bud. I had seated myself with the boys for our noon meal, when I missed him. 'Where's old Bud?' I asked. 'Why, don't you know? Bud died two days ago and we are burying him tomorrow at – cemetery outside the town." There was a settled gloom I had never encountered before in their company, and hardly a word spoken during the remainder of our lunch hour. The day after the funeral I was with them again.

'Well,' I said, 'you planted poor old Bud all right I suppose?' A prolonged silence followed and crossing looks took place. I sensed they had a grievance. Had I spoken irreverently of Bud? I asked myself. No: they knew me and that I respected Bud.

'Grave-diggers? Bah,' one of the company suddenly ejaculated, 'Call 'emselves grave-diggers. Why they could not hold a job as navvies. The walls out of plumb, the angles all awry – Bah! If poor Bud could have got up he would have kicked the backside of the bloke who dug his grave.' And soon I was listening to spade artists bemoaning the fate of their fellow craftsman having to lie in an ill-wrought vault. I thought a lot that afternoon of the artist that is in all men and at night in my shack I wrote a poem about an imaginary place where all could exercise their gifts for the gratification of all and not for hireling's pay.

I had just finished this when I got a letter from my journalist friend's widow. She had arrived back from her sad journeying and set herself to the task of keeping herself and two bonny bairns by the pen, and had eventually been able to visit Capri, which she had known in happier days. From Capri then came her letter wishing me well. I slipped a Legend Poem, dedicated to her, into my letter in response to hers. And in due course the postman delivered me a novel founded on my poem, called *The Splendid Failure*, which she had written. My ego got a big bump up as I realized I had helped somebody to do something.

However, here at Heswall, divided by the romantic Dee from Wales and its mountains, I gave myself over to an orgy of meditations. I had cut and fixed a circular flight of diminishing steps in a garden, leading from one flat to another, when the owner's little daughter came out of the house and I coaxed her to walk up the steps. No one, not even I, the builder, had walked up them as yet. Standing on the topmost step she so touched my fancy that I wrote the following dedicated to

DAPHNE

We tore the stone from Mother Earth
To build our circled stairs,
The centre ones we shaped alone,
The outer ones in pairs.
At length the work accomplished,
The studied height attained –
One thing alone seemed wanting,
The climax still remained.
When, from the house, an Angel came,
Mounted our stony pile
And, silhouetted 'gainst the sky,
Stood balanced for a while,
With elfin hat and smiling eyes,
Her wee mouth sweetly pursed,
She looked a picture for the gods
If ever one was birthed.
Ah! proud the craftsman who can see
His work so sanctified,
And, pinnacled against the sky,
Innocence deified.
Ah! Maiden sweet, whose lissom feet,
My stony stairs first trod,
So, may the years throughout thy life
Prove stepping-stones to God.

This little effusion I next day offered to the child's mother, who brought out her camera and we again posed the bairn standing on the topmost step, a copy of which photograph I treasure along with a copy of *The Oxford Book of English Verse* with which I was presented by her fond parents. It was my first and a most appropriate return for my versifying.

But when I was now evicted from my wheeled castle I sought sanctuary in the bungalow home of a friend, situate in the same field. A few weeks after, however, they moved into a brick-built house away from the sight of Wales and the Dee and I stayed on at the bungalow as tenant. But a couple of weeks only had passed when, again I got the inevitable blue paper. My new home was condemned as 'not being it for habitation'. It had been the home for a dozen or more soldiers for the four years of the war but was not fit for an hardened old, hermit like myself who wished to be alone, finding ample happiness in his own thoughts and company.

I therefore removed myself over to Liverpool. Here a long spell out of work brought me to have to live on a dole of twelve shillings per week. Of this I paid seven shillings and sixpence for a room, leaving four shillings and sixpence for food, coal, clothing and sundries.

Result – when 21 few days before Christmas 1933 I did get employment in a local stone yard, I was so run down that a week of it laid me low. My doctor certified me as suffering from sillicosis, the dreaded masons' disease, accelerated by malnutrition. A few years back the government had inaugurated a scheme whereby a fund was formed from payments, part by stone-working firms, and part by the national exchequer, from which a pension was provided for any man suffering through the inhaling of stone dust in the course of his work. I was X-rayed three times to find out if I had really contracted the complaint, and then told I hadn't it bad enough for the pension or even a part of the pension. Instead, I was certified to have the form of heart disease known as angina pectoris, and would never work again. I fancy I have cut my last stone. Sometimes only with difficulty can I breathe, and the ten shillings per week reduced sick pay which I now live on is a ghastly joke.

By returning to the Deeside again, I saved five shillings in rent per week and slept in a tent I had erected in the adjoining field where I had my workshop. This I called my studio. It sounded more posh. In my teens I had worked on a fine stone-built mansion for Mr. Ismay the founder of the White Star Line of Steamers, at Dawpool, a few miles from Heswall. I saw it advertised for demolition. At the sale a splendid example of my craft, a hanging Minstrel's Gallery in red sandstone, was one of the lots. There were no bidders as it seemed too intricate a piece of work to be dismantled without breakage. But a son of the founder eventually purchased the lower hall, on condition it could be taken down and delivered at his home in the South of England.

I was offered £100 to do this work. But it entailed hurling the top portion, some ten tons comprising one hundred stones, to the ground to be smashed beyond recognition. This vandalism made me jib. As a craftsman I realized the loving care the operatives had taken to produce such fine work. Eventually I acquired the top portion for £50 off my contract price and carefully took it down, but where to put it. Looking round I found and rented a small plot of ground. Here I removed my spoils and packed them up. Around them I built a shed. But, when I had finished my shed, I couldn't get into it on account of the stonework. I now had to move the stones out and, making a doorway and window in the sides of my erection, I used it as a workshop. And here and around it reposes the beautiful stonework which I had hopes of incorporating into an ideal dreamer's home.

However only a month back a great gale demolished my tent, and I was driven to live in my studio. And a week after taking up my residence here, an official entered, sent by the Urban District Council, to tell me to get out or they would send their men to demolish it 'as not being fit for human habitation'.

During my enforced retirement from physical toil, I was

not idle. I was still able to use the lighter hammer and tools for carving, and when my chest pains were not too severe, I would spend an hour or two a day, carving a sandstone garden ornament out of the local rock, for my own garden. By the sale now and again of one of these for a few shillings, I was able to eke out an existence with the aid of my ten shillings per week from the National Health insurance fund. Sometimes instead of a sale I made a deal. In the local hostelry I frequented, I was sitting one day when in limped Hoggy, my pal, a bus conductor. 'What's the matter, Matey?' I asked, to be told that he had purchased a pair of rubber-soled boots the day before, and not being used to rubber, the constant running up and down stairs to collect fares had crippled him.

'And now I'm going home to change them for my old ones. No more rubber-soled boots for me,' he said, adding, 'What size do you take Fred?' 'Eights', I replied. 'Well,' he said, 'I've always wanted something to remember you by. Will you give me a squirrel for the boots?' Would I? I was almost bootless, so I quickly closed with the offer.

Another time, I was getting desperate. My larder was almost empty, so shouldering a rockery rabbit, I climbed the hill to the nearest inn and tendered my last coppers for a drink. I had resolved on becoming a pedlar of my wares and was wondering where to make a start to try to find a buyer for my rabbit, when, in walked a local 'sportsman'. 'Any luck?' I asked. 'Yes', and he turned out from a capacious inner pocket a freshly shot bunny. 'I've a rabbit myself' I said, showing him my stony model. 'Swop?' he said. I had already hungered for his rabbit, and the deal was soon made and I sped down the hill to cook his kill. And it was only after I'd had my fill that I considered what a rotten 'salesman' I would make, to swop eight hours toil for a one-shilling market price rabbit.

For some months now I had been quietly engaged in producing 'a book'. A year previous I had entered a competition a publishing firm was running for the most interesting autobiography, open to any one in the world. The hours and hours I spent, the scraps of paper I used, the writing and re-writing, the whole work, was getting me down. Eventually I finished it and sent it off. Months passed and it was returned as 'not suitable'. I approached a well-known writer in a week-end paper – 'Would he please run through my story and advise me if 'twas worth while hoping to get it produced?' 'Yes', he would. Months again passed and at last I wrote requesting the manuscripts return. At length it came back with no comments. Again I sent it off to a Labour M.P. representing my craft. Back again, after many weeks, it came. Again, no comments. I now felt as though I were doomed to die without seeing my work in the Press. I am under no delusion as to the shortness of my days through the shortness of my breath. Eventually I saw the prize-winning story which had beaten mine, reviewed in the *Sunday Referee* by a novelist and critic named John Brophy. 'There are many men of a humbler sphere in life who could have written a more interesting life,' or words to that effect, was his concluding criticism. This heartened me to write to him. 'Would he read etc?' He would. He did. Four days after I had sent it off I heard from him.

I have finished. My literary Godfather is 'seeing this thing through' for me. With the writing of this book I feel that my useful life is almost finished. But I have lived and I have no regrets.

THE END

ABOUT THE EDITORS

Ron Noon was, until retirement, Senior Lecturer in History at Liverpool John Moores University, and has had a career-long interest in research into the Liverpool labour movement. His most recent publication, jointly written with Sam Davies, is 'The rank-and-file in the 1911 Liverpool General Transport Strike', in *Labour History Review*, vol. 79, no. 1, 2014.

Sam Davies is Professor of History at Liverpool John Moores University. His most recently published book is *County Borough Elections in England and Wales, 1919-38: A Comparative Analysis, Volume 4, Exeter to Hull* (Ashgate, 2013).